HMS Vanguard
1944-1960
Britain's Last Battleship

Neil McCart

Published by Maritime Books, Lodge Hill, Liskeard,Cornwall PL14 4EL

Printed and bound in the United Kingdom by J.H. Haynes & Co. Ltd., Sparkford

Contents

Introduction

Without doubt *HMS Vanguard*, with her flared bow, forward sheer, towering superstructure and her raked-topped funnels, was the most handsome battleship ever built for the Royal Navy. In 1939, when plans were first mooted for the construction of this one-off vessel, no one could foresee the demise of the battleship as the Navy's capital ship. Nevertheless, in September 1945 when the Second World War ended, and *Vanguard* was still languishing in the builder's shipyard, there were those who thought that she was already a white elephant, and that she would prove to be a liability. In the age of nuclear weapons and fast aircraft carriers which would soon be flying off jet aircraft with speeds of over 500 knots and ranges of up to 950 miles, what role could the battleship have?

When, in 1946, *Vanguard* was eventually commissioned she was given a prestige role - that of a "Royal Yacht". It was the illness and subsequent death of King George VI which prevented her from keeping the role in the years that followed. There were even plans that she should carry Sir Winston Churchill across the Atlantic Ocean for a summit meeting with the President of the United States. There is something rather sad in seeing this leviathan of the sea, the last of the Royal Navy's magnificent battleships, being reduced to carrying VIPs round the world, or acting as a floating saluting platform for state visits to this country of foreign heads of state. The reality of the situation was, however, that the day of the battleship was over and, in the words of a distinguished US Navy Admiral, it was as "dead as the dodo".

Over the years countless numbers of books have traced the careers of the earlier battleships of the Royal Navy, through both the First and Second World Wars, but little has been written about *Vanguard*. Perhaps this is because, during her short career, she never had occasion to fire her guns in anger. I hope this book helps to set the record straight as for the first time *Vanguard's* story is told.

Neil McCart
Cheltenham
November 2001

An Uncertain Start - 1939 to 1945

Britain's last battleship takes shape. *Vanguard's* hull lay on the stocks for three years as building priority was given to the aircraft carrier *HMS Indefatigable*. In this view the trunks for X and Y gun turrets are under construction.   *(Author's collection)*

On Thursday 2 October 1941, at the shipyard of John Brown & Company on the River Clyde, the keel was laid for what was to be the Royal Navy's last battleship. This Clydebank yard had seen many such leviathans take to the water, including the illustrious names *Hindustan, Inflexible, Tiger, Repulse*, the mighty *Hood* and, in February 1940, the great battleship *Duke of York* which was launched from the company's East Yard. In October 1941, so strong was the image of the battleship as the Royal Navy's ultimate weapon, that few people could have predicted that this vessel, with her massive 15-inch guns, would be the last capital ship of her type.

The story of this particular battleship goes back to February 1939, when the Director of Naval Construction suggested that the 15-inch gun turrets, which had been removed from the light battlecruisers *Courageous* and *Glorious* in the 1920's when they

were converted to aircraft carriers, could be used to arm a "one-off" battleship which could be built quickly before the four more powerful Lion-class that had been proposed. At that time the Second World War was still some six months away, and only a few aviation enthusiasts could foresee that the war, which everyone knew was inevitable, would be one in which the aircraft carrier would succeed the battleship as the fleet's capital ship.

It was May 1940 before the design of the new battleship was approved and 12 months later, in May 1941, came the catastrophic loss of the battlecruiser *Hood*. The public relief which followed the destruction of *Bismarck* tended to overshadow the decisive role played by the Fleet Air Arm in both the hunting and sinking of the mighty German battleship. Later that year, however, in December 1941, the sinking of the battleship *Prince of Wales* and the battlecruiser

Repulse off the coast of Malaya, for the loss of just a handful of Japanese aircraft, brought home the helplessness of these huge vessels when faced with overwhelming air power. The aircraft carrier which could project its offensive power over hundreds of miles had succeeded the battleship.

There is no doubt that within the Admiralty this fundamental change in maritime warfare was acknowledged, with the cancellation of the four projected Lion-class battleships and priority given to the completion of the Illustrious and Implacable classes of fleet aircraft carriers, as well as the light fleet aircraft carriers of the Colossus and Majestic classes. The order for the new "one-off" battleship had been placed on 14 March 1941, and she became John Brown & Company's yard number 567. With the keel being laid seven months later, it appeared that the Navy would acquire just one more new such vessel before the end of the Second World War. During 1942, despite the fact that the completion of the new battleship had become a priority second only to the aircraft carrier *Indefatigable*, with emergency repairs on damaged ships to carry out, and with shortages of skilled labour

and materials, progress was slow. In April 1942 it was clear that yard number 567 would not be ready before the summer of 1945, but in those days nobody could have predicted the sudden end to the war in the Far East and it was generally thought that the battleship would see war service east of Suez. One young schoolboy, Keith Wilkinson, who would later undergo training on board *Vanguard*, remembers that his school in County Durham ran a campaign to collect discarded newspapers as their contribution towards the cost of what they were told would be, "a superior battleship, built in Britain's image." He remembers that the more newspapers one collected, the higher up the school's promotion ladder one could ascend, and that his efforts resulted in him becoming a "General", complete with a paper badge.

In early 1944, following the completion of *Indefatigable*, yard number 567 was given top priority by the Admiralty and on Thursday 30 November that year she was ready for launching. It was appropriate that the Royal Navy's newest, biggest and last great battleship should have a royal sponsor. HRH Princess Elizabeth who, at just 18 years old, was car-

An excellent shot of *Vanguard's* flat transom stern as she lies on the stocks at John Brown's Clydeside shipyard.

(Author's collection)

HMS Vanguard was launched by HRH Princess Elizabeth on Thursday 30 November 1944, shown here on the launching platform just seconds after releasing the launching mechanism. *(Author's collection)*

Flying the John Brown house-flag and the Union Flag *HMS Vanguard* thunders down the slipway and into the waters of the River Clyde.

(Imperial War Museum A26625)

4

rying out her first major public engagement by launching the ship. After travelling north to the Clydeside shipyard she met the First Sea Lord, Admiral of the Fleet Sir Andrew Cunningham, the First Lord of the Admiralty, A. V. Alexander, and the Managing Director of John Brown & Company, Stephen Pigott. As well as other dignitaries a number of shipyard workers and their families were presented to the Princess, whilst around the yard the open girders of the tall gantries surrounding the slipway made good vantage points for swarms of adventurous workers who whistled and cheered their approval. Before the ceremony the Princess walked the full length of the battleship's keel, among the chocks which held her upright and the huge piles of chain cable, towards the stern where she was shown the electrically operated release mechanism. From there Princess Elizabeth made her way to the launching platform at the stem of the ship, and after a short religious service she pressed the button which released the vessel and, at the same time she let go the cord holding a bottle of Empire red wine which smashed against the hull. In a clear voice which was amplified around the yard by loudspeakers, she pronounced, "I name this ship *Vanguard*. May God bless her and all who sail in her." There was a short pause before the great hull moved slowly away, gathering speed as it thundered down the slipway into

the River Clyde. As the stern took to the water the White Ensign was run up while the chain cables ran out with a rushing sound, throwing up clouds of dirty red dust which almost hid the ship from view. Then, as *Vanguard* was towed to the fitting-out berth, the Princess and other occupants of the launching platform left for the traditional luncheon which always followed such an event.

During the luncheon the Princess was presented with a diamond brooch, fashioned as a "Rose of England", which she said would always remind her of the first important public duty she undertook. Of *Vanguard* she remarked: "I am very proud to come here to launch this truly magnificent addition to the Royal Navy. You may be sure I shall always follow the movements of this fine ship and of all who serve in her with the greatest possible interest. When I first saw her I found it hard to realise that this vast structure, now safely afloat, is the work of men's hands. The men and women of this shipyard may indeed feel proud of this evidence of their patience, their skill, and their hard work through many months. They must surely have put something into her which is part of the staunchness of our race."

The First Lord of the Admiralty, A. V. Alexander, who had been born in 1885 when battleships reigned supreme in the fleet, perhaps unwittingly reminded

After the launch *Vanguard* is towed away to the fitting-out berth. The area where her armour belt will be fitted can be seen on the hull. *(Author's collection)*

Vanguard's superstructure takes shape. Here the trunks for the starboard 5.25-inch guns are under construction.
(Ian Johnston/National Archives of Scotland)

Vanguard's after funnel is lifted into place.　　　　　　*(Ian Johnston/National Archives of Scotland)*

By the autumn of 1945 X turret is almost complete and Y turret is under construction.

(Ian Johnston/National Archives of Scotland)

Both X and Y turrets have been completed, but the secondary armament has yet to be fitted.

(Ian Johnston/National Archives of Scotland)

his audience of just how the role of these mighty ships had been reduced to that of a floating battery for shore bombardments, when he said, "This ship is a challenge to the minds of people who have thought, and who still think, that the role and the day of the battleship have ended. The experience of naval minds has proved the contrary. The work of the battleships in the open sea and for close bombardment under proper air protection in narrow waters has been a revelation. I am persuaded that a ship of the calibre and equipment that this ship will have will be a formidable central factor in any naval task force which can be devised for the future." Strangely, however, although detailed reports of the ceremony appeared in the national newspapers two days later, and the recording of the ceremony was broadcast on the BBC's Home Service, the vagaries of the censorship rules meant that the name of the new battleship could not be published.

Despite the fact that completion of *Vanguard* was now a priority, it was becoming clear that she would not be ready for sea before the spring of 1946. However, in August 1944, under the command of Commander (E) F. B. C. Smith RN, the first key naval personnel were appointed to the ship and on the last day of February 1945, with the defeat of Germany only weeks away, it was considered safe to make public the battleship's name and the fact that she was being built at Clydebank. Few other details were released, however, and there was a great deal of spec-

ulation in the press that she would be armed with nine 16-inch guns. Seven months later *Vanguard* was in the news once again, but this time in a report that there had been an explosion on board which had claimed the lives of three workmen. Although damage to the ship was superficial, it seemed that methane gas from sediment on the bed of the fitting-out basin had seeped into the ship and in some compartments had accumulated into a highly explosive mixture which had been ignited by cutting torches. Just four weeks later, on Monday 15 October 1945, six weeks after the end of the Second World War, *Vanguard's* first commanding officer, Captain W. G. Agnew CB CVO DSO RN, was appointed to the ship.

Captain Agnew, who was a gunnery specialist, was born in the closing years of the 19th century, when battleships were the undisputed capital ships of the Fleet, and he had entered the Royal Navy as a cadet in 1912. During the Second World War he had commanded the cruiser *Aurora* in the Mediterranean, and in 1941-42, when Britain's fortunes were at a low ebb, his dashing exploits against Italian convoys and surface forces did a great deal to improve flagging morale at home. In 1943 he commanded the 12th Cruiser Squadron, then in January 1944 he was appointed to command the Navy's gunnery school, *HMS Excellent*, at Whale Island, Portsmouth.

It was to be another six months, however, before the battleship was ready for sea.

A fine view of Vanguard as she lies alongside her fitting-out berth in John Brown's yard, almost ready to go to sea.

(Ian Johnston/National Archives of Scotland)

Chapter Two

Completion and Trials - 1945 to 1946

With a displacement tonnage of 44,500, overall length of 814ft - 4in and a draft of 34ft - 10in, *Vanguard* was easily the biggest battleship ever built for the Royal Navy. In general her design followed that of the earlier King George V class, and although it had been intended to give her a straight bow and level forecastle, seagoing experience with the latter had demonstrated the need for extra freeboard forward. A cutaway bow with more flare was added to her overall length. Her armour protection was similar to that in the King George V class, but her main armament was unique and although it has been widely stated that her eight 15-inch guns were originally fitted in the light battlecruisers *Glorious* and *Courageous*, this is not true. Her four main turrets did in fact come from these vessels and, after modernisation at John Brown's Scotstoun yard, their thicker armour and increased elevation (which provided extra range) proved very successful. The eight 15-inch guns themselves had previously been fitted in the battleships *Queen Elizabeth, Ramillies, Royal Sovereign, Resolution* and the monitor *Erebus*, whose single gun had come from *Royal Sovereign*. The Royal Navy's 15-inch gun log, which was immaculately kept by the staff at the Royal Navy's

Ordnance Depot at Priddy's Hard, Gosport shows that the stock of 15-inch guns were, during refits, regularly removed, refurbished and eventually replaced in other vessels. The eight guns were fitted in four twin turrets, two forward and two aft. In addition *Vanguard* was fitted with 16 5.25-inch high-angle guns in eight twin turrets, as well as 58 40mm Bofors guns.

Vanguard was a quadruple-screw ship, with her engine rooms and boiler rooms arranged in four separate units, and although each unit operated independently, cross connection facilities were provided. She was powered by four sets of Parson's single-reduction geared steam turbines which developed 130,000 SHP which gave her a maximum speed of 30 knots. The steam was provided by eight, oil-fired, Admiralty Three Drum boilers (two to each of the four boiler rooms), which supplied steam at 700°F and 400psi. The auxiliary machinery included four 450kW diesel generators, and four 480kW turbo alternators.

As to her accommodation *Vanguard* was built with central messing dining halls for senior and junior ratings, an ice cream and soda bar, a bookstall, a library and a fully equipped laundry. All the bathrooms were fitted with stainless steel washbasins and showers, and the ship was equipped with heating for service in

During the forenoon of 2 May 1946, eight months after the end of the Second World War, *HMS Vanguard* finally left the builder's yard to make her passage down the River Clyde to Greenock. As always the departure of a prestigious new ship was of great interest to the local people.
(Author's collection)

Vanguard starts her move down river towards Greenock.   *(Maritime Photo Library)*

Another shot of the battleship as, guided by tugs, she steams slowly down the River Clyde.   *(Author's collection)*

Watched by a lone spectator *Vanguard* passes the Erskine Ferry which, in those days, was a local beauty spot.

(Author's collection)

The battleship passes Port Glasgow on her way to the Tail of the Bank.

(Author's collection)

Arctic conditions and with some limited air-conditioning for her expected service in tropical waters. With a peacetime complement of 1,893 officers and men *Vanguard* was clearly going to be, in an austere post-war Britain, an expensive commitment for whichever government was in power. As the last of her kind she would always be a target for those who wanted to cut defence costs. The total cost to build *Vanguard*, including the expenditure necessary for modernisation and adaptation of the gun mountings, had been approximately £11,000,000. However, in 1946, as she emerged from the builder's yard, with her flared bow, her towering superstructure, her raked-topped twin funnels and her flat transom stern, she looked every inch the capital ship.

In a navy that was reducing its manpower by up to 26 per cent, the manning of a capital ship the size of *Vanguard* was bound to present the Admiralty with a problem. In March 1946 drafts of men travelled north to Clydeside to join the ship. One such draft included a number of Royal Marines, among them Fred Russell, who remembers his first day on board the battleship: "When we arrived at John Brown's shipyard, there, alongside the wharf was the mighty *Vanguard*. Whilst I was waiting to embark I can recall standing there and looking up at this huge, powerful, but grace-ful battleship, which was to be my home for almost two years. Once on board I found spaciousness everywhere, with wide passageways, large messdecks and bathrooms and, for the first time in my service, a dining hall which was separate from the messdeck."

On Tuesday 26 March 1946 it was officially announced from Buckingham Palace that the King and Queen, accompanied by the Princesses Elizabeth and Margaret, would visit South Africa in February the following year, and that they would make the voyage in *Vanguard*. It was clear from this that the new battleship was to be the Royal Navy's prestige vessel. The main draft of seamen and stokers arrived from the Royal Naval Barracks, Portsmouth, on 28 March and later that day, at 1700, Divisions were held on the quarterdeck when Captain Agnew read the Commissioning Warrant and the White Ensign was hoisted. For the rest of the month, however, *Vanguard* remained alongside the fitting-out berth while last minute preparations were made to get her ready for sea. It was at 0800 on Thursday 2 May 1946 that she was finally ready to move downstream to start her initial trials. Three hours later, with the pilot embarked, the order "Obey Telegraphs" went down to personnel manning the main machinery compartments. With hands manning the ship, *Vanguard* slipped her berth at

The wardroom onboard *HMS Vanguard*.   *(Author's collection)*

One of the Chief Petty Officers' messes. *(Author's collection)*

1124 and, for the first time, under her own steam she prepared to negotiate the River Clyde as she steamed slowly down river. The weather for the occasion was perfect, with scarcely a breath of wind. Many local people turned out to watch this historical event as the last in a long line of the Royal Navy's mighty battle-ships made for the open sea. The 14-mile passage of the narrow waterway was made easier by the fact that the channel had recently been dredged for the Cunard liners *Queen Elizabeth* and the *Queen Mary*. By 1300 she had reached Dumbarton. Half an hour later she was off Port Glasgow and at 1411 she slipped the last of the tugs that had guided her down river before commencing compass adjustment and turning trials. She anchored at exactly 1900 off Greenock, close to the giant ocean liner *Queen Elizabeth* which itself was at anchor and refitting after her war service.

Over the next nine days stores and ammunition were embarked, last-minute cleaning and polishing was endlessly carried out and guns' crews for both the main and the secondary armament were drilled. On 8 May BBC and press representatives visited the ship. The ship's company prepared her for the formal commissioning service which was scheduled for Sunday 12 May which would be attended by HRH Princess Elizabeth. After an all-night train journey from London, Princess Elizabeth arrived at Greenock on the Sunday morning to board the royal barge at Prince's Pier for the short journey out to the battleship which, being dressed overall and with the ship's company manning the huge superstructure, looked immaculate. As the Princess boarded her personal standard was broken from the gaff, and Royal Marine buglers sounded a royal salute. The first ceremony was the formal commissioning of the ship which took the form of a short religious service on the quarter-deck. The Princess then went to the Chapel of St Andrew onboard for a dedication service before undertaking a tour of the ship she had launched 18 months earlier. Finally, after lunching with Captain Agnew and senior officers, at 1440, accompanied by the cheers of the ship's company who were manning ship, the Princess disembarked into the royal barge waiting by the starboard gangway.

Four days after the royal visit, at 0915 on Thursday 16 May, *Vanguard* weighed anchor to start four days of trials in the Firth of Clyde. During the first morning at sea the engineers put the main propulsion machinery through its paces as they carried out full-power trials. These were followed by gun blast, turning and radar trials, the latter in conjunction with RAF Mosquito aircraft. During the morning of Monday 20 May, with the ship in the North Atlantic off the Skerries, anti-submarine exercises were carried out

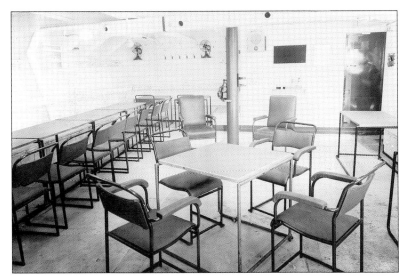

A Junior Ratings' mess deck, showing the punkah louvre ventilation, the hammock hooks and the rather spartan furniture of the day.

(Author's collection)

Another Junior Ratings' messdeck showing the small kit lockers and the long wooden mess table. Again the facilities are very basic compared to today's standards.

(Author's collection)

One of the Junior Ratings' dining halls in *Vanguard*. The central messing system was a great improvement on the general messing system where cooks of the mess collected the food from the galley and meals were eaten on the mess decks.

(Author's collection)

and as soon as these were completed the battleship set course for Liverpool. Later that afternoon, with the ship's company manning ship, she steamed up the River Mersey to secure in Liverpool's Gladstone Graving Dock where her underwater hull could be scraped and painted.

During the four weeks spent in dry dock at Liverpool the opportunity was taken to grant leave to the ship's company, and *Vanguard* herself was a constant source of fascination to many visiting dignitaries. Among those who visited the ship during this period were General Sir William Slim, the commandant of the Imperial Defence College, an all-party delegation of Members of Parliament, and civic dignitaries from the city of Liverpool. By mid-June, however, stores and ammunition had been embarked, and the ship was afloat in the Gladstone Dock where inclining trials had been carried out. Finally, at 1045 on Monday 17 June, she slipped her mooring ropes and the tugs began the task of manoeuvring her into the River Mersey. By 1600 that day she had disembarked the pilot and course was set for the Firth of Clyde. It was to be her base for the official trials which began the next morning when she carried out exercises with two submarines. On Tuesday 25 June she carried out air-defence exercises with Fleet Air Arm Seafires, and three days later she started 48-hours of full-power trials over the Arran measured mile. This measured mile was much favoured by shipping companies and by the Royal Navy for running various types of trials with their ships, as the sheltered waters enabled speeds and fuel consumption to be accurately recorded. It was marked by two sets of long white poles sited on high ground which were exactly one nautical mile apart. However, after working up to full speed *Vanguard* approached the start of the mile to find that there was no sign of the vital white poles. Much to the dismay of those on *Vanguard's* bridge, at the other end of the run the second pole was also missing and the battleship's first attempt to calculate her speeds was abandoned! On investigation it was found that a wartime Polish Army camp had been situated on the shore at exactly the point of the measured mile, and at the end of the war when the camp had been evacuated, as well as dismantling the huts it was assumed that the poles were part of the camp and they too had been cut down and taken away. Fortunately, they were soon replaced and *Vanguard* was able to make her runs at full power along the measured mile. The main engines developed 136,000 SHP, giving the ship a speed of 31.57 knots, which was well in excess of her design requirements and must have given great satisfaction to both the builders and to Captain Agnew.

Trials continued until mid-July, and on Tuesday 16

July, when she was in the Irish Sea north of Bishop Rock, she carried out a full-scale air-defence exercise during which she was subjected to mock attacks by Fleet Air Arm Fireflies and RAF Anson and Mosquito aircraft. Whatever the official conclusions, those involved could not fail to be reminded of the vulnerability of battleships to air attack. Next morning before the city of Plymouth had properly woken up, with her decks fully manned *Vanguard* steamed into harbour and entered No 10 dry dock at Devonport Dockyard. During her stay in Devonport a number of adjustments were carried out to the main propulsion machinery, and on the afternoon of Thursday 8 August she steamed out of harbour to carry out her final trials before setting course for Portsmouth. Next day, at 1010, she rendezvoused with *HMS Duke of York* and saluted the flag of the C-in-C Home Fleet, Admiral Sir Neville Syfret, who was flying his flag in the older battleship. Later that day, at 1630, *Vanguard* anchored at Spithead where, on behalf of the Admiralty, Captain Agnew formally accepted the battleship from John Brown & Company. Her entry into harbour was delayed for three days, as severe gales and heavy rain lashed the south coast. Finally, with the weather having improved, at just after midday on Monday 12 August she was able to weigh anchor and steam up harbour with her decks fully manned to secure alongside South Railway Jetty. For almost four months, whilst the dockyard fitted her out for the royal tour of South Africa, which was due to start in February 1947, the battleship remained firmly alongside this prestigious berth.

In order to convert the battleship for service as a "Royal Yacht" the apartments and offices which were designed for use by an Admiral and his staff, and which were situated at the after end of the superstructure on the shelter deck, were to be converted into a royal suite. This meant that structural alterations were kept to a minimum so that they could be completed by early December, when *Vanguard* was due to undertake a trial cruise. The Admiral's dining, sleeping and day cabins, the Chief of Staff's suite and the range of offices were adapted for use by the Royal Family. On the port side were the King and Queen's suites, with adjacent working apartments for their domestic staff. The King's dining cabin was on the starboard side. Forward of this, and also on the starboard side, were the cabins for the Princesses, which were both very small. Aft of the dining cabin the King's private secretary was provided with an apartment, with other members of staff being accommodated on the deck above. The decoration of the apartments was kept simple, with most bulkheads being painted in cream with most of the furniture being taken from the elderly and

A stoker tends the oil-fuel sprayers in B boiler room. Steam for the main engines was supplied by eight Admiralty Three Drum boilers. *(Author's collection)*

One of *Vanguard's* four engine room starting platforms.

Looking aft to Vanguard's bridge superstructure with A and B turrets in the foreground.   *(Author's collection)*

An impressive close-up of the forward 15-inch guns.   *(Author's collection)*

disused Royal Yacht, *Victoria & Albert*. The main feature was the dining table which could seat 22, with its own suite of chairs and sideboards, which would be used for state functions. In order to be able to fly the Royal Standard the battleship's mainmast was lengthened by the addition of a pole mast, which could be floodlit when the occasion demanded it. One of the ship's motor boats, a 45-foot diesel-driven picket boat, was converted for use as a royal barge. In order to provide a saluting platform for the royal party the twin 40mm Bofors guns, which were situated on top of "B" turret, were removed and a platform, complete with glass windshields, was built in their place. To complete the work *Vanguard* herself was repainted in a lighter grey colour.

By Monday 25 November 1946 the battleship had embarked her full complement of men for the Royal Tour, which included the Band of the Portsmouth Division, Royal Marines, under Major Vivian Dunn, the Director of Music. A group of Sea Cadets and Sea Scouts, who would act as messengers during the tour

also joined. The additional numbers strained all the accommodation to its limits, and camp beds became a feature of both wardroom and lower deck life. One Royal Marine remembers that his camp bed was actually situated in a working alleyway, and recalls being instructed to cover himself with a sheet at all times when "turned in" as the Queen was known to go "walkabout" at all times of the day and evening.

Finally, with all the work having been completed, at 0715 on Wednesday 4 December 1946 *Vanguard* slipped quietly out of Portsmouth Harbour for a 16-day trial cruise into the Atlantic Ocean. After leaving the Channel she set course south for warmer waters which took her as far south as Madeira and the Canary Islands. After spending two days in the vicinity of the Atlantic Islands she steamed north to berth alongside Gibraltar's south mole during the afternoon of Friday 13 December. During the weekend alongside some members of the ship's company were able to do last-minute duty-free Christmas shopping, whilst others tried the local brew, only to find it too strong for them.

HMS Vanguard at anchor off Greenock. In the background, and framed by the guns of Y turret, is the Cunard liner *Queen Elizabeth* which was being refitted following her war service.   *(Author's collection)*

Back on board, the ship was opened to the public and there was an official reception for 300 guests, which was designed to test the ship's services for the state functions which would be held on board during the forthcoming royal tour. For the guests there was added interest when the Royal Marines Band Beat Retreat on the quarterdeck, and supplemented their usual range of musical instruments with Scottish bagpipes. The weekend alongside ended on the morning of Monday 16 December when, in company with the destroyer *Chivalrous*, *Vanguard* left harbour and set course for home. After an uneventful voyage, and a night anchored at Spithead, she secured alongside South Railway Jetty on the morning of Friday 20 December 1946. She was now deemed ready to undertake her Royal Tour.

Left: On 12 May 1946, HRH Princess Elizabeth, the battleship's royal sponsor, visited *Vanguard* whilst she was anchored off Greenock. In this photograph the Princess is being guided around the ship by Captain Agnew.

(Author's collection)

Overleaf: Princess Elizabeth is cheered by the ship's company as she leaves the battleship.

(Author's collection)

Vanguard running her trials in the Firth of Clyde. *(Author's collection)*

An impressive view of the battleship on her trials. Y turret is trained on the camera.

(Imperial War Museum A31248)

On 16 July 1946, when *Vanguard* was in the Irish Sea north of Bishop Rock, she carried out an air defence exercise in which she was subjected to mock attacks by Fleet Air Arm and RAF aircraft. In this photograph two Mosquitoes "attack" the battleship.

(Imperial War Museum A31201)

Another photograph of the same exercise showing two aircraft strafing a target astern of *Vanguard*.

(Imperial War Museum A31200)

On Wednesday 17 July 1946, *Vanguard* arrived in Devonport Dockyard from her trials, and is seen here entering No 10 dry dock. Continual steaming at high speed had taken its toll on her paintwork.

(Syd Goodman collection)

Chapter Three

The Royal Tour - January to May 1947

The Royal Tour of South Africa early in 1947 was to be King George VI's last overseas journey. It is said that the idea of a State Visit to the Union had first been suggested by General Jan Smuts, the country's Prime Minister, during his wartime visits to England. At Westminster there were some back-bench grumblings about the proposed visit, but otherwise both Clement Attlee's Government and the King were keen to reaffirm the link between the Crown and the Union. In addition the King wanted to thank the South African citizens for their efforts on behalf of the Allied cause during the Second World War. The tour, which would cover some 23,000 miles in a period of 12 weeks, would be strenuous and was significant in that it marked the debut of the Princesses Elizabeth and Margaret as Royal Ambassadors overseas. With the elderly Royal Yacht, *Victoria & Albert*, having carried out her last royal duties in July 1939, and having been out of service since the start of the Second World War, *Vanguard* was the obvious choice for the role, for not only had she been launched by Princess Elizabeth, but she had not yet taken on any operational role. So, in mid-January 1947, with the ship's company having taken their seasonal leave, the battleship was ready to embark her royal guests.

The last week of January 1947 was marked by icy weather and blizzards which hit most of the country on 24 January and which continued with little respite for the rest of the month. The south coast suffered heavily with snow drifts of up to 20 feet deep in parts, and with many villages being cut off for considerable periods of time. The severity of the weather emphasised the parlous state of the country's fuel situation as the nation slowly recovered from the crippling cost of the war, and many areas of the country were badly hit by power cuts. Air temperatures were recorded as being the lowest since 1870 and on 29 January the Thames and Medway Rivers both froze over, as did the sea in Folkestone Harbour. This then was the scene as, during the afternoon of Friday 31 January

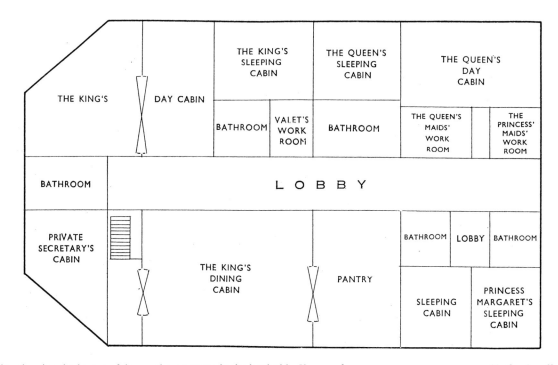

A plan showing the layout of the royal apartments in the battleship *Vanguard*.   *(Author's collection)*

King George VI's dining cabin in *HMS Vanguard*. The furniture was taken from the redundant royal yacht *Victoria & Albert*. *(Author's collection)*

The King's day cabin. *(Author's collection)*

The Queen's day cabin.
(Author's collection)

The Queen's sleeping cabin.
(Author's collection)

Princess Margaret's sleeping cabin.
(Author's collection)

1947, the King, Queen and the two Princesses boarded the Royal Train at London's Waterloo Station for their journey to Portsmouth.

Boy Seaman John Hucker remembers the day well: "We had to get up early, very early, to wash down the quarterdeck and sweep several inches of snow from the awnings. It was a great relief when we sailed south." At 1625 the royal party arrived at the city's Harbour Station where, despite the deep snow and freezing weather, they were given an enthusiastic welcome. The grey, cold day did not stop the people of Portsmouth from turning out to line the Station Approach and The Hard as the cavalcade of cars drove the short distance to South Railway Jetty. On board *Vanguard* the duty watch had taken the canvas shrouds from the heavy guns and other pieces of equipment which had provided protection from the heavy overnight snowfalls, and working parties swept the snow from the upper decks and the jetty in preparation for laying the red carpet. At 1500 all work in the dockyard stopped for the day and, as the Royal Train drew into the station, the battleship was dressed overall and the ship's company manned every available inch of the upper deck on the port side of the ship. On South Railway Jetty the approach of the Royal Family was heralded by the cheers of the crowds, and as the King stepped from his car the guard, which was drawn from the naval barracks, gave a royal salute. After inspecting the guard the royal passengers, who were accompanied by Queen Mary, the Princess Royal and the Duke of Gloucester, climbed the gangway where they were piped on board and received by Captain Agnew. That afternoon they met all the ship's officers, as well as the heads of dockyard departments who had been involved with the construction of the royal apartments. Later in the day Queen Mary, the Princess Royal and Duke of Gloucester left the ship and the King entertained the C-in-C Portsmouth, Admiral Sir Geoffrey Layton, Rear-Admiral Lord Mountbatten, Lady Mountbatten and Captain Agnew at dinner. That night the Royal Standard flying at *Vanguard's* masthead was floodlit, but heavy overnight snowfalls meant that few people saw the battleship as preparations for her departure began at 0300. At 0630 the pilot was embarked and half an hour later the ship's company manned ship. At exactly 0720 the battleship cast off from South Railway Jetty. Preceded by the Trinity House vessel *Patricia* and an escort of MTBs, the great battleship steamed slowly out of harbour past Fort Blockhouse and the Round Tower, where crowds of intrepid sightseers had braved the freezing conditions to wave goodbye. From Portsmouth they sailed

The Royal Guard who lined Portsmouth Harbour's Station Approach and The Hard march out from the dockyard with the Royal Marines Band. On an icy-cold day oilskins and greatcoats were rig-of-the-day. *(Tony Perrett)*

Sailors lining The Hard Present Arms as the Royal Family pass by.   *(Tony Perrett)*

Meanwhile, at South Railway Jetty............   *(Tony Perrett)*

...And on *Vanguard*'s quarterdeck, snow and slush is swept away in preparation for the Royal Family's arrival.

(Tony Perrett)

After clearing the decks of ice and snow the ship's company wait for formal proceedings to get under way.

(Tony Perrett)

With the ship's company manning ship the King inspects the Royal Guard of Honour on South Railway Jetty. All the men have an array of war medal ribbons on their No 1 uniforms.   *(Tony Perrett)*

to a rendezvous with the Home Fleet some 20 miles south-west of St Catherine's Head, *Vanguard* was escorted by the destroyers *Obedient, Offa, Opportune, Orwell* and *Rotherham*. Under a heavily overcast sky the escort moved into line ahead about a mile in advance of the battleship. Three miles beyond the Nab Tower the destroyers formed a screen, and the course was altered to south-west. The screen was achieved from line ahead in a graceful manoeuvre, with *Offa* and *Opportune* turning away to starboard, and *Obedient* and *Orwell* turning to port. The four vessels each described a huge S manoeuvre while *Rotherham* continued ahead at reduced speed. *Vanguard*, her massive superstructure looming grey in the haze almost a mile away from her escorts, ploughed the green sea, with waves breaking heavily over her bows. Eight miles beyond the Nab Tower the sky was ominously dark and *Offa* was forced to deviate from the formation to pass a merchant ship, but as they reached the rendezvous point the dim shapes of the Home Fleet loomed into sight. First the battleship *Nelson*, followed by *Duke of York* and the aircraft carrier *Implacable*, with the smaller units being obscured by the gloom.

As *Vanguard* and her formation neared the units of the Home Fleet, the five escorting destroyers turned round and steamed past the battleships in line ahead. To complete the picture RAF Beaufighters, Mosquitoes and Sunderland aircraft circled overhead

in salute. Finally, as the destroyer flotilla steamed astern the King sent the following message to them by signal lamp: "Thank you for your escort and kind message of good wishes."

When *Vanguard* was within a mile of the Home Fleet, the 17 units of which lay formed in two lines, through the murky light flashes of their saluting guns could be seen as they fired a 21-gun salute. Then, as the fleet, led by *Duke of York* and *Nelson*, steamed in two columns of line ahead to meet the *Vanguard*, the edge of the dark blanket of cloud lifted, transforming the Channel to a brilliant green colour which formed a perfect setting. Dressed with masthead flags and with their ships' companies lining the guard rails, at 1100 exactly *Vanguard* entered the two lines of warships in an impressive demonstration of seamanship for which the Royal Navy is second to none. The scene only marred slightly by a small shabby, merchantman, belching black smoke from its funnel, steamed through the formation. As the Home Fleet saluted *Vanguard*, from Portsmouth came a signal giving the position of a floating mine, a leftover from the Second World War, which had been sighted south of Durlstone Head, about two miles from the battleship's course. It was a reminder that the escort had to keep a sharp lookout during the voyage.

As soon as *Vanguard* had passed between the lines of Home Fleet ships she prepared for a "first" for the Royal Navy, and one which was an important step in

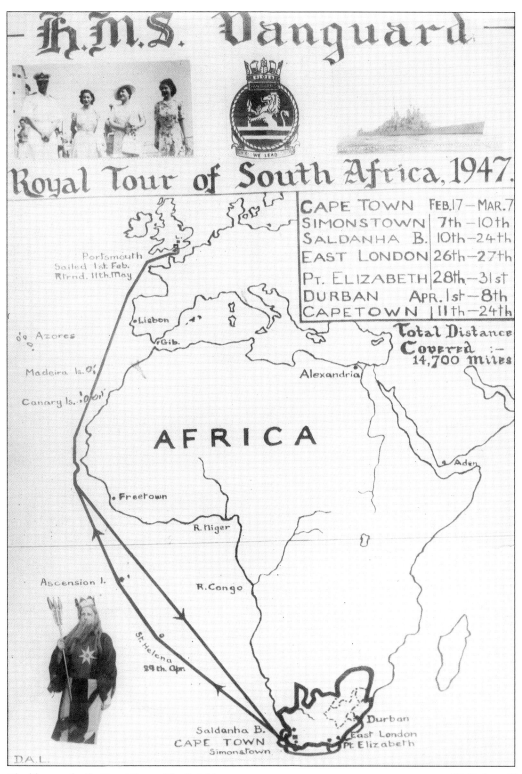

H.M.S. Vanguard

Royal Tour of South Africa, 1947.

CAPE TOWN	FEB.17 – MAR.7
SIMONSTOWN	7th –10th
SALDANHA B.	10th –24th
EAST LONDON	26th –27th
Pt. ELIZABETH	28th –31st
DURBAN	APR. 1st – 8th
CAPETOWN	11th –24th

Total Distance Covered :– 14,700 miles

Portsmouth
Sailed 1st. Feb.
Rtrnd. 11th.May

Azores
Madeira Is.
Canary Is.

Lisbon
Gib.
Alexandria

AFRICA

Aden

Freetown
R. Niger

Ascension I.
R. Congo

St. Helena
29th. Apr.

Durban
East London
Pt. Elizabeth

Saldanha B.
CAPE TOWN
Simonstown

D.A.L.

The itinerary for the Royal Tour of South Africa.   *(F. W. Russell)*

the development of naval aviation. That morning one of five Sikorsky R4 Hoverfly helicopters, which made up one-fifth of the Navy's helicopter strength, took off from Portland to fly over the Home Fleet. The small flight had carried out many spectacular trials with ships in the area but on that day south Dorset was experiencing blinding snowstorms. This did not deter the pilot, Lieutenant K. M. Reed, and at 1000 he set off in a blizzard past Portland Bill, heading south to look for *Vanguard* and her escorts. After 15 minutes he flew into bright sunlight and he soon spotted the warships as they steamed in formation. Then, at 1135, with *Vanguard's* guard rails still in place, with ventilation trunkings and hatches protruding from the landing area and some of the battleship's personnel wearing caps with chin straps up, the helicopter landed on the *Vanguard's* quarterdeck. Today flight deck officers and helicopter crews would never dream of landing without taking full safety precautions, but this was a ground-breaking flight and after collecting mail and photographic film the pilot took off again just six minutes later to fly to Gosport where photographs were developed, printed, and sent to the local newspaper for the evening editions. Although this feat does not sound spectacular today, in the late 1940s it was considered almost revolutionary and it was

an impressive demonstration of the helicopter's versatility.

Two hours later the French battleship *Richelieu*, flying the flag of Rear-Admiral F. P. Jourdin, and two French destroyers, loomed into sight to pay the French Navy's tribute to the King. Once again, the Royal Family took the salute from the "B" turret saluting platform as heavy seas broke over the bows of both battleships and drenched everyone who was on the open decks. By 1520, however, *Richelieu* and her two escorting destroyers had turned away northwards. Onboard *Vanguard* the duty watch secured deck fittings and closed all hatches against the rough weather which had been forecast for the following 24 hours. That night the battleship and her escorting dcstroyer, *St James*, steamed into Force 10 southwesterly gales as they ploughed their way across the Bay of Biscay. It was said that very little was eaten in the royal dining suite that evening and that all the Royal Family retired early to bed. As *Vanguard* pushed through huge waves many of the weather decks were placed out of bounds and even the Royal Marines on quarterdeck lifebuoy sentry duty during the middle and morning watches were stood down as they were in danger of being swept overboard themselves. In spite of the weather, however, the battleship

At 1135 on Saturday 1 February 1947 came an important event for the Royal Navy when a Sikorsky R4 Hoverfly helicopter landed on the quarterdeck. Note the lack of safety precautions which would appal today's Flight Deck Officers. *HMS Implacable* can be seen in the background.

(Richard Holdaway)

Lieutenant K. M. Reed preparing to take off from *Vanguard's* quarterdeck. His visit to the battleship lasted for only six minutes before he left to deliver mail and film to Gosport. *(Colin Bowden)*

The escorting aircraft carrier *HMS Implacable* as seen from *Vanguard's* quarterdeck. *(Authors collection)*

held her course and speed, but the much smaller *St James* was forced to reduce speed to 14 knots and soon she fell astern of *Vanguard*. Daylight brought little respite from the severe gales, and as the battleship continued into the heavy seas the Royal Family spent most of their time in their apartments. She was, however, making steady progress southwards and the air and sea temperatures were rising steadily. The King, Queen and Princesses were able to watch the seas breaking over the escorting units. Even the aircraft carrier *Implacable* was forced to ease her speed when one of her booms was damaged by the enormous waves. Marine Colin Bowden, who was just 15 years old at the time, remembers going onto *Vanguard's* quarterdeck, which was under water from time to time, and watching the great aircraft carrier "digging-in" as the huge waves broke over her flight deck. As the squadron steamed down the Portuguese coast the sloops *Bartolomeu Dias* and *Dao Ibez*, under the command of Commodore Da Forca, steamed out from Lisbon to salute *Vanguard*, and in reply to the Portuguese vessel's message the King signalled back,

"I thank you for your gesture of friendship. The Queen and I are much touched by your sailing out to greet us in this weather."

Despite the severe weather, during the night of 3 February one of the ship's cats, Minnie, gave birth to two kittens, which were quickly adopted by the ship's company.

By the morning of Tuesday 4 February *Vanguard* had entered warm sunshine and calmer seas off the coast of southern Portugal, and with wind speeds down to 10 knots and the sea running a low westerly swell, everything was much more comfortable on board. With the temperature having risen to 64°F the Royal Family were soon out on deck to watch mail and 450lb of bread being transferred by jackstay to the *St James*. Her galleys having been flooded during the storm her staff had been unable to cook or bake for almost 24 hours. Once the evolution had been completed the destroyer, her ship's company manning the guard rails, steamed slowly past *Vanguard* before setting course for Lisbon. Before she left the King signalled to her, "Thank you for your escort and kind

...And *Vanguard* as seen from *Implacable's* flight deck. The ships experienced severe weather conditions during the first few days of the passage to South Africa for the Royal Tour. *(Imperial War Museum Neg A31297)*

message. You have kept up valiantly in the bad weather. Hope you will get dry and be enjoying hot food again soon. The Queen and I send you best wishes."

As *St James* sailed north once again *Vanguard* and *Implacable* were joined by the destroyer *St Kitts* from Gibraltar.

That the severe weather had taken its toll on the appetites of the Royal Family is testified to by ex-Royal Marine "Jackie" Poole, whose duty it was to stand guard on the royal apartments: "The trip across the Bay of Biscay had been a bit on the rough side and things were getting more settled when I had the forenoon watch guarding the royal apartments. Just before the end of my watch a servant came out of the galley with a tray and headed for the King's apartment. However, he returned almost immediately still carrying the tray and I made some comment on the speed of the service. To this the man told me that the King didn't feel up to food, and had just wanted a drink. I jokingly said, "Good, more for me." What a shock I got when he gave me the tray with a piece of fish, and bread and butter, it tasted delicious. Mind you the treat was never repeated, but I used to get a cup of tea half way through my watch."

On the morning of Wednesday 5 February the battleship and her escorts passed between the islands of Tenerife and Gran Canaria, where they were just five miles from the town of Santa Cruz. The King and Queen visited *Vanguard's* main galley where they were shown the "new" machine which actually sliced and buttered bread, and witnessed the preparation of the midday meal - which was Lancashire Hot Pot, followed by date pudding and custard.

Next day the ship's company changed into white tropical rig, but a proposed visit to *Implacable* was postponed because of a heavy swell although the carrier was able to carry out flying exercises a short distance from *Vanguard*. At 0600 on Friday 7 February, the force passed Cape Verde lighthouse and just over four hours later both the battleship and the carrier stopped in relatively calm waters 30 miles west of the Gambia River whilst the Royal Family were transferred by royal barge to the aircraft carrier, watched by a number of small local fishing boats who had put out to see the squadron as it passed the Gambian coast. The King was received on board *Implacable* by a Royal Marines guard of honour, then with the Queen and the Princesses he watched a flying display by six of the carrier's Seafires and Fireflies. Afterwards, still in overalls and working gear, the ship's company mustered on the flight deck where the Queen made a short speech. After lunch the royal party visited the cruisers *Cleopatra* and *Diadem* and the destroyer *St Kitts*, all of which were due to hand over the escort on

The King and Queen are piped over the side as they leave *Vanguard's* quarterdeck to visit the aircraft carrier *Implacable*.
(Richard Holdaway)

Two Fireflies from *Implacable* fly over *Vanguard* while the cruiser *Nigeria* joins the escort.

(Imperial War Museum A31301)

the next day. Finally, having toured all three ships they returned to *Vanguard,* which then resumed her voyage south. That evening the weather was warm enough for her passengers to sit out under the quarterdeck awning to watch the film, "Odd Man Out".

John Hucker remembers the voyage south thus: "Dress of the day whilst at sea was very informal and we usually wore No 8s, which were just coming into issue, and gym shoes, which was very unusual in the Navy of those days. Before we sailed, Captain Agnew had cleared lower deck and told us that this was probably the only time the family would have a proper holiday so we were not to take advantage of our privileged position and should give them plenty of space. The after superstructure of *Vanguard* had been altered to incorporate a royal sun deck and a kind of patio area. A few of us Boys were formed into a small Division called Royal Top Men, with a CPO Button in charge. It was our job to keep the royal sun deck clean and tidy, put up and take down awnings and side screens and to generally be on hand to carry out any other duties. All the paintwork was a very expensive and shiny enamel grey for this special trip and we had to keep it clean by regularly touching it up and cleaning it with a liquid soap called 'teepol', which was an early form of detergent. One day, whilst I was touching up the grey enamel paintwork on the mushroom vents on the sun deck, the King came up and, without warning, leaned back and rested his hands on some of my fresh paintwork. I remember he remarked, 'Bloody Navy, always painting.' I helped him to wipe the paint off his hands with white spirit and a piece of cotton waste, and he soon forgot the incident. I also recall all the guard rails in our area had been specially made of brass wire rope and we had to polish them every morning, which was a difficult job on spun wire. As Royal Top Men, one of our 'unofficial perks' was the fact that a large jar of boiled sweets was kept on a table for the Royal Family, but with sweets still rationed at that time, when no one was looking the temptation was too great and we all 'liberated' one or two sweets now and again.'

During the afternoon of Saturday 8 February the cruiser *Nigeria* joined the squadron to take over the escort, with *Implacable's* aircraft mounting a fly-past over the *Vanguard*. After which, the departing *Implacable, Cleopatra, Diadem* and *St Kitts*, with their ships' companies cheering ship, steamed past the battleship before setting course for Freetown. By the next day, with *Vanguard* about 60 miles north of the equator and over half way to the Cape, the weather was hot, with clear blue skies and seas. That evening traditional ceremonies were observed when the ship stopped to allow CPO H. T. Brown in the guise of "Dolphinius Clerk to the Court of King Neptune" to "board" the ship to announce that King Neptune him-

The two Princesses meet Minnie, *Vanguard's* dining hall cat who, during the night of 3 February, gave birth to two kittens.

(J.W. Hucker)

self would convene his court on the battleship's quarterdeck the next day. The announcement was followed by a magnificent fireworks display on the forecastle as *Vanguard* continued her steady progress south. On the following morning, at 0900 precisely, the ceremony opened with the parading of the royal guard and Commander John Lamb, together with the Master at Arms, stood ready to "receive" the visitors. These preliminary proceedings were watched by the Royal Family from the superstructure overlooking the quarterdeck, but the procession soon moved up to the starboard side of the forecastle where a canvas pool and a stage had been built for the occasion. As the King was on his way to the pool he happened to pass a stranded 24-inch manila rope lying on the deck, which he was told was the main brace. "Then have it spliced", was his reply! Needless to say, the order to issue a second tot of rum was always popular. First to fall victim to King Neptune were the King's Equerries, Lt-Cdr Peter Ashmore and Wing Commander Peter Townsend. The two Princesses were excused the

ducking chair, receiving only a light powdering and a "pill", which looked very much like a glace cherry, before being presented with their certificates. Following this the bears showed no mercy and Major Vivian Dunn, the BBC Correspondent Frank Gillard and representatives from all departments of the ship's company received duckings, including Major R. C. de M. Leathes, the officer commanding the Royal Marines Detachment. The fun and games continued until just after 1100 when the ducking pool was left in place as a ship's company swimming pool. *Vanguard* increased speed to 17 knots again to continue her voyage.

During the next two days *Vanguard* entered the region of the south-east trade winds, where a long swell gave the ship a heavy roll which continued most of the way to Cape Town. On Friday 14 February the King and Queen donned boiler suits and toured the ship's main propulsion machinery compartments, where the temperatures were in excess of 100°F. Later they visited the Stokers' dining hall and dined in the

King Neptune and his "consort" sit between the King and Queen as the Crossing the Line ceremony and duckings get under way.
(Andy Lucas)

The Princesses Elizabeth and Margaret escaped a ducking, and instead they received only a light powdering from the "barber".
(Andy Lucas)

The Royal Family look on as members of the ship's company receive their duckings. Every available space, including A and B turrets, are occupied by spectators.

(Richard Holdaway - above: Andy Lucas - below)

wardroom. With the ship nearing her destination excitement on board mounted and during the morning of Saturday 15 February Captain Agnew stopped the ship for over four hours, during which time she drifted with the currents, in order that the hull and superstructure could be washed and some of the paintwork touched up. By now the battleship was just under 800 miles north-west of Cape Town, and Sunderland flying boats of the South African Air Force were able to rendezvous with the squadron to augment the escort. The last full day at sea was marked by a south-westerly gale which was reminiscent of the Bay of Biscay as the squadron was joined by the sloops *Actaeon* and *Nereide*. At 0630 on Monday 17 February, the South African frigates *Good Hope, Natal* and *Transvaal* steamed out from Simonstown to join the escort and, by 0815 *Vanguard* lay outside Cape Town Harbour to embark the pilot.

The day was bright, calm and cloudless as the battleship, dressed overall and with her decks manned by the ship's company all in white tropical rig, looked immaculate as she was manoeuvred slowly to her berth in the city's Duncan Dock. The paintwork on her hull recalled the stormy passage of the first few days of the voyage. Ashore, thousands of people thronged the area around the docks and the roads were lined with schoolchildren waving Union flags. At 0940 the Prime Minister, General Smuts, and the Governor-General were greeted by Captain Agnew and the Royal Marines band played the national anthems of the two countries, "God Save The King!"and "Die Stem van Suid Afrika." Soon afterwards the King, wearing the uniform of an Admiral of the Fleet, and accompanied by the Queen and two Princesses, disembarked to the tune of "Will Ye No Come Back Again?" at the start of the first state visit of a reigning monarch to the Union of South Africa.

After attending official functions at Cape Town and Simon's Town, the Royal Family returned to *Vanguard* on the evening of 19 February and after touring the wine region of Paarl and Stellenbosch, at 1600 on Friday 21 February they boarded a train at Duncan Dock, bound for Port Elizabeth and the start of their eight-week tour of the country. Meanwhile the

A magnificent view of *Vanguard* as she steams south towards Cape Town.   *(Imperial War Museum FL20865)*

HMS Vanguard arrives at Cape Town on the morning of Monday 17 February 1947. *(Author's collection)*

Soon after the battleship's arrival the Royal Family disembarked for their tour of South Africa. In this view they are being received by the Governor-General of the Union. The Royal Marines Guard of Honour is paraded on the quarterdeck

.

(Andy Lucas)

HMS Vanguard alongside her berth in Cape Town's Duncan Dock. The special seating arrangements which were constructed for the Royal Family's welcoming ceremony are still in place. *(J.W. Hucker)*

Vanguard floodlit at Cape Town. *(Richard Holdaway)*

battleship's ship's company could look forward to 14 days of relaxation in Cape Town before carrying out their own, more limited, tour of South Africa's main ports. During the first weekend at Cape Town the ship was opened to visitors and during eight hours no less than 17,300 people flocked on board to view the battleship. On the jetty there was a drill display by the Royal Marines and the band Beat Retreat to appreciative audiences. However, at just after 1430 on the last day of February everyone was brought back down to earth when the fire alarms sounded as an electrical fire broke out in the starboard computer room, and thick black smoke poured out of the compartment. Fortunately, the fire was extinguished quickly, but power was temporarily lost throughout the ship. That evening, with smoke having made the dining halls unusable, meals were served on the messdecks. Although the damage was soon repaired it was clear that eventually permanent repairs would have to be carried out by Portsmouth Dockyard.

During the days alongside at Cape Town parties were given for 750 children and the South African Governor-General visited the ship. Finally however, after having been held up for 24 hours by strong winds, at 0700 on Friday 7 March *Vanguard* left harbour to carry out gunnery practice. It was a reminder to everyone onboard that they were still an operational warship. They then steamed the short distance to Simons Bay where, at midday the same day, they anchored. During the weekend many members of the ship's company took trains back to Cape Town for the more lively attractions of the city. On Sunday 9 March it was back to business when she weighed anchor to carry out full-power trials and radar exercises en route to the remote anchorage of Saldanha Bay, 100 miles north of Cape Town on the Atlantic coast. That same afternoon, after anchoring out of the public eye, the ship's company got down to two weeks of renovating the ship, holding regattas and saving some money for the forthcoming runs ashore. During the stay the cruiser *Nigeria* arrived for a short stopover, as did the sloop *Actaeon* and the South African frigates *Good Hope* and *Transvaal*, which allowed for fleet regattas to be held. Most days, however, were spent washing and painting the ship's hull and superstructure, but at least the weather was warm and sunny.

Finally, after embarking Vice-Admiral Sir Clement Moody, the C-in-C South Atlantic, on Monday 24 March *Vanguard* weighed anchor and in company with the *Transvaal*, she steamed round the Cape of Good Hope to anchor off Mossel Bay on the continent's south coast. During the passage she carried out a 5.25-inch throw-off shoot at *Actaeon*. The C-in-C was disembarked off Simonstown before the battle-

ship took part in a night encounter exercise. Off Mossel Bay, however, although the weather was fine, the heavy swell which is a feature of the area made boatwork difficult and the deputy mayor of the town and nine of his dignitaries were *Vanguard's* only visitors. Most of the residents who wanted to see the battleship had to be content with cruising round the ship. The ship's company were unable to get ashore. Finally, at just after 1400 on the same afternoon the battleship departed. The next scheduled stop, three hours later, was the attractive harbour of Knysna, 50 miles east of Mossel Bay, where it had been intended to anchor for two hours, but a heavy sea breaking on the Bar prevented the battleship from lying off. The several hundred sightseers who had gathered on the town's East Heads had to content themselves with the magnificent sight of *Vanguard* steaming at slow speed about a mile offshore. The following day she sailed in close to Port Elizabeth and through Bird Island Passage. Captain Agnew had hoped that during the afternoon he would be able to anchor off Port Alfred at the mouth of the Kowie River. However, the continuing heavy sea prevented this and small boats were unable to leave harbour. She continued on up the coast, and at 1820 anchored off East London. Next day the continuing heavy swell meant that boat traffic between ship and shore was suspended and although Captain Agnew was able to visit the town's mayor, there was no shore leave. During the day sightseers came out in fairly large vessels to see *Vanguard* and Colin Bowden remembers that at one stage while the Royal Marines Band Beat Retreat on the quarterdeck local boats circled quite close around the ship with a floating audience. On the lower deck it had, however, been proposed to grant shore leave to CPOs and POs but as this had not materialized to any great extent for 19 days, there were murmurs of discontent on some messdecks. Commander Lamb soon got to hear of this and after bringing it to Captain Agnew's attention, at 1730 the lower deck was cleared and Captain Agnew addressed the ship's company. He assured them that in future there would be no such restrictions, but he was obviously unable to do anything about the crowded living conditions on board. Colin Bowden remembers hearing a few, "Rhubarb, Rhubarb" comments, but following the talk nothing more was heard from the few discontented members of the ship's company and *Vanguard* weighed anchor at 1830 to set course back to Port Elizabeth. This "incident" has received little publicity over the years, but in 1992 one journalist described it as a "slight case of mutiny", which it never was.

At 0900 on Friday 28 March, the battleship arrived off Port Elizabeth in thick fog and, on the advice of the port authority, she anchored two miles from the end of the harbour breakwater. Once again a heavy swell prevented the ship's own boats from getting to and from shore, but the port authority put one of their large tugs at Captain Agnew's disposal and in the fine weather a "make and mend" was piped with shore leave being granted to all but the duty watch. The first tug got away from the ship safely carrying 600 officers and men, but on returning to the ship the increased swell threatened to carry away the tug's wires and the tug master refused to land any more men. For those liberty men stranded ashore there was the problem of accommodation and Colin Bowden and a number of others spent the night in a local school.

Next morning, with the wind and the sea having decreased, Captain Agnew was able to give leave to the other watch and at 1100 700 men were landed. That afternoon, however, the swell once again increased to such an extent that, again, the tug was unable to lie alongside the battleship. During the weekend dances and picnics were organised ashore and, needless to say, they were all well attended, contributing to a high level of morale on board when *Vanguard* weighed anchor on the morning of Monday 31 March.

Next day, at 1425, *Vanguard* cleared the breakwater entrance to Durban Harbour where she was greeted by the opera singer Perla Gibson, the famous "Lady in White", who was well known to all who had served in the wartime East Indies Fleet. The ship was soon secured alongside M jetty in Durban Docks, which fortunately, meant that there did not need to be any restrictions on shore leave. The hospitality in the city proved almost overwhelming. During the three days that the battleship was opened to visitors over 26,500 people came on board to look round and the ship's company entertained some 500 local children at a party on board. After seven days in Durban it was time to return to Cape Town again. She left harbour to the accompaniment of a selection of sentimental songs from Perla Gibson. During the three-day passage *Vanguard* had final "battles" with *Actaeon, Good Hope* and *Transvaal*, and after passing close to the town of Hermanus, south-east of Cape Town, she arrived alongside J berth in Duncan Dock at 0945 on Friday 11 April.

The second stay in Cape Town was marked by more rain and less in the way of official entertainment. Two ship's company dances were held ashore and one on board, all of which proved to be very popular. A further 9,500 people came to look over the Navy's latest battleship.

On the return passage, as well as her royal passen-

gers, *Vanguard* would carry a consignment of gold bullion for the Bank of England. This arrived alongside the ship at 0800 on Thursday 17 April. Ron Poole, who was on duty as gangway sentry, remembers the escort arriving at the ship: "The leading vehicle of the Police convoy was a motor cycle with a side car that was equipped with a machine-gun, and there were others similarly armed as well as armoured cars. It was quite a formidable force. The two bullion vans came to a halt only a few yards from where I was standing, and when their doors opened out swarmed armed policemen who unloaded the boxes of gold on to the jetty. One of the police officers then asked the officer of the watch to provide a guard, who, pointing at me, replied, 'Its all right I've got a Royal Marine to look after it all.' It was clear that the South Africans were amazed, they had a small army equipped with machine-guns and armoured cars and all I had was my 1917 vintage Lee Enfield rifle. Unknown to them it wasn't even loaded." In fact the gold was perfectly secure for there was a large working party of officers and men ready and waiting to hoist it on board, so it was soon stowed safely away.

Three days later the ship was dressed overall and the decks were manned to welcome the Royal Family back on board. The next day, Monday 21 April 1947, was Princess Elizabeth's 21st birthday. To celebrate the event the Royal Family were entertained by the city of Cape Town where the Princess made her famous radio broadcast to the Empire. In the evening there was a huge fireworks display on the jetty. On the next day the royal baggage was embarked and the ship was placed under "Sailing Orders". At 1600 the next day, with all preparations having been completed, the mooring lines were slipped and, slowly but surely, *Vanguard* moved away from the jetty to the accompaniment of a choir and bands, and cheering crowds who had come to wave goodbye. As the bow of the battleship turned towards the harbour mouth the well-wishers surged down to the edge of the jetty, and just over half an hour after leaving, *Vanguard* and *Nigeria* rendezvoused with *Good Hope, Natal* and *Transvaal*, who provided the escort for two hours before turning back to Simon's Town.

After five days at sea, early on the morning of 29 April landfall was made and the two warships anchored off Jamestown, St Helena, where the whole population of just under 5,000 turned out to welcome the royal visitors who went ashore for a four-hour visit. By 1740, however, the battleship and cruiser were under way again. Two days later they hove to off Georgetown, Ascension Island, where many islanders came out in small boats to greet the Royal Family while overhead a USAAF Flying Fortress from the

The Royal Family leave *Vanguard* in the Royal Barge for their visit to Jamestown, St Helena. *(J.W. Hucker)*

As *Vanguard* steams slowly past Georgetown, Ascension Island, the Royal Family wait on the quarterdeck as small boats make their way out to the battleship. *(J.W. Hucker)*

The Queen and the two Princesses leave *Vanguard* in No.1 cutter to visit the aircraft carrier *Triumph*.

island's air base circled in salute. Two days after leaving Ascension Island behind *Vanguard* and *Nigeria* rendezvoused with the aircraft carrier *Triumph* and the destroyer *Raider*, both of which had been temporarily detached from the Mediterranean Fleet to take over the escort from *Nigeria*, which left for Freetown. At 0648 on Wednesday 7 May *Vanguard*, which had now also collected the cruisers *Cleopatra* and *Diadem* to supplement her escort, passed within five miles of Las Palmas, Gran Canaria. In mid-morning the Queen and Princesses visited *Triumph* and inspected Divisions on the carrier's flight deck. However, a proposed visit to *Raider* was cancelled because of a heavy swell. Unfortunately, the King, who was suffering from what transpired to be Buerger's disease, was unable to join them. Thus, with *Vanguard* flying the King's Standard and *Triumph* flying the Queen's Standard, it was the first time at sea that both Royal Standards had been flown together. Next day *Triumph* and *Raider* parted company to return to the Mediterranean.

By the evening of Friday 9 May *Vanguard* was off Cape Finisterre in a heavy sea and high winds, but it did not stop the two Princesses from visiting one of the ship's boiler rooms and an engine room, where they took control of the battleship's engine room throttles and then steered the ship from the lower steering position for an hour of manoeuvres. At 1000 on Sunday 11 May, as *Vanguard* steamed up the

Channel, the lower deck was cleared and the men mustered on or around the quarterdeck where the King thanked the ship's company for all their efforts during the tour and, as an additional bonus, he granted all of them an additional three days' leave. In his address the King remarked: "The Queen and I and the Princesses will always look back on our time spent on board *Vanguard* with the greatest pleasure. We wish you all good luck and a happy leave." On behalf of the officers and men of the battleship Captain Agnew presented farewell gifts, for the King a wallet and brooches for the Queen and Princesses, each bearing *Vanguard's* crest. At 1700 on Sunday 11 May *Cleopatra* and *Diadem* took their leave of *Vanguard* and the Trinity House vessel *Patricia* took station ahead of the battleship as she passed the Nab Tower and steamed into the Solent. From early that morning thousands of people had been flocking to the vantage points in the area. It was estimated that almost 500,000 people were gathered along the seafront between Old Portsmouth and South Parade Pier. At 1730 five MTBs took up the escort and at 1750 *Vanguard*, with her ship's company lining the rails, steamed along Southsea Front, past the Round Tower and into Portsmouth Harbour. With the vast crowds cheering and waving there was no solemnity to the occasion and the Royal Family, who were on "B" turret saluting platform, waved cheerfully back. Colin

Bowden, in the Royal Marines Band, remembers that, "It was a fine evening, we played all the way into harbour and while the ship was turned prior to berthing." At 1800 the ship was turned off North Slip Jetty and manoeuvred back down harbour, to secure alongside South Railway Jetty exactly 50 minutes later.

After shaking hands with all *Vanguard's* officers, the Royal Family disembarked at 1000 on Monday 12 May 1947, the tour having been an unqualified success. Politically it did nothing to help the moderate South African Prime Minister, General Smuts, in his 1948 election campaign when his party lost to the hard-line Nationalist Party - to the future detriment of South Africa. However, it is said that King George VI greatly enjoyed his voyage in *Vanguard*, and his Equerry later recalled the pleasure he derived from being on board a battleship once again.

For *Vanguard* herself there lay ahead a long refit and many months alongside in dockyard hands before she went to sea again. There also remained the problem of finding a role for the battleship in the post-war nuclear age where aircraft had taken on the main strike role of the fleet at sea.

Escorted by the cruisers *Cleopatra* and *Diadem* and flying the Royal Standard, *Vanguard* steams up Channel towards Spithead at the end of the royal tour. *(Author's collection)*

With her upper decks manned *Vanguard* steams through the Solent to Portsmouth, in better weather than when she left three months earlier. *(Author's collection)*

During the late afternoon of Sunday 11 May 1947 *Vanguard* arrived back at Portsmouth. In this photograph the battleship steams past Southsea seafront, escorted by *MTB 2016*. *(Maritime Photo Library)*

Cheered by the ship's company, who manned every available space, the Royal Family disembark from *Vanguard*. On the raised dias in front of the crowd is the BBC broadcaster Richard Dimbleby.

(Imperial War Museum HL39198)

With the Royal Tour over *Vanguard* lies alongside South Railway Jetty. In place of the Royal Standard the White Ensign is flying at the specially constructed masthead.   *(Maritime Photo Library)*

In Search of a Role
May 1947 to September 1951

wo days after arriving back in Portsmouth from South Africa *Vanguard's* cargo of gold bullion was unloaded and dispatched to the Bank of England's London vaults. Following this, at 0930 on Thursday 29 May 1947, there was a change of command when Captain F. R. Parham DSO RN joined the ship to take over from the recently promoted Rear-Admiral Agnew, who left later in the day to take up an appointment at the Admiralty. That same day it was announced that Vanguard was to be sent to Devonport to refit, during which permanent repairs would be carried out to her fire-damaged computer room. It was also announced that, because of the refit, the battleship would be unable to take part in the Fleet Review on the Clyde that summer, and that the C-in-C Home Fleet would fly his flag in the battleship *Duke of York*. Captain Parham had first gone to sea in 1917 in the battleship *Malaya*, and he had subsequently specialised in gunnery. On the outbreak of war in 1939 he was commanding the Tribal-class destroyer *Gurkha*, which was bombed and sunk during the Norwegian campaign. In autumn 1942, after being promoted Captain, he took command of *Belfast* at Devonport following her long 34-month period in dockyard hands having been mined off the Firth of Forth in November 1939. He commanded the cruiser for two years, during which time *Belfast* took part in the action which resulted in the sinking of the German battlecruiser *Scharnhorst* in the Barents Sea, and later the bombardment of the Normandy coastal defences on D-Day.

During *Vanguard's* stay in Portsmouth the furniture which had been taken from *Victoria & Albert* was removed from the battleship and returned to the eld-

On 26 June 1947 *Vanguard* left Portsmouth for Devonport where she was destined to remain, in dockyard hands and manned by a care and maintenance party, for over a year. Here she is shown leaving Portsmouth Harbour.

(Maritime Photo Library)

Vanguard leaving Devonport on 31 August 1948, to anchor in Mevagissey Bay, Cornwall, before undertaking her post-refit trials and sailing for the Mediterranean. She still has the mainmast extension for, at that time, it was thought that she would carry the Royal Family on a proposed visit to New Zealand and Australia.   *(Maritime Photo Library)*

erly Royal Yacht, although the royal apartments were left otherwise intact.

On Friday 20 June the C-in-C Portsmouth, Admiral Lord Fraser, paid a short visit to the battleship and six days later, at 0800 on Thursday 26 June, *Vanguard* left Portsmouth Harbour for Devonport, which was to be her new home port. That same evening, at 1930, she anchored in Plymouth Sound. Next day she steamed up harbour to secure alongside 6 & 7 wharves in the dockyard. Five days later, with the ship having been taken over by the dockyard, her ship's company was reduced to a smaller care and maintenance complement as *Vanguard* herself was destined to remain in the dockyard until the end of August 1948.

The large reductions in manpower which had been made in the Royal Navy in 1946 and 1947, mainly by the discharge of "Hostilities Only" ratings, would have made the manning of *Vanguard* difficult.

In the summer of 1948 it was announced that the battleship would undertake her second Royal Tour. This time she was to carry the King, Queen and Princess Margaret to New Zealand and Australia for a tour which would last from January to July 1949. The royal party was scheduled to leave London on 27 January 1949 and embark in *Vanguard* at Devonport later in the day. She was due to sail during the same afternoon. This time she would make a transatlantic crossing to arrive at Colon, Panama, on 9 February.

She would then make a transit of the Panama Canal and arrive at Wellington on 28 February, where the Royal Family would disembark. During their tour of New Zealand it was intended that *Vanguard* would make her own mini-tour of the country's seaports, before re-embarking her royal passengers (at the end of March) for a passage to New Zealand's Bay of Islands and Sydney in Australia. Finally, on 11 June 1949, the Royal Family were to rejoin *Vanguard* at Fremantle, with the long voyage home being made via Cape Town.

First, however, the battleship had to recommission and on Thursday 18 March 1948, with her ship's company having been brought back almost to full strength, they were inspected by the C-in-C Plymouth, Admiral Sir Robert Burnett. This was followed by an address by Captain Parham who gave the men a rough outline of the ship's itinerary which would begin with a shakedown cruise to the Mediterranean. Before she put to sea, however, the battleship remained a magnet for VIPs. At 1050 on Saturday 1 May 1948 the Prime Minister, Clement Attlee, together with the First Lord of the Admiralty, Viscount Hall, spent just over an hour on board inspecting the work which had started on the royal apartments and discussing with Captain Parham arrangements for their refurbishment. By the end of July 1948, with the fitting out of the royal accommo-

Two of the ninety boy seamen who were drafted to *Vanguard* for the proposed royal tour of 1949 are seen here painting the anchor cables whilst the battleship is moored in Portland Harbour in September 1948. Note the King's saluting platform is still in place on top of B turret.

(Frank McGuinness)

dation almost complete, the battleship had carried out her basin trials, and at 1440 on the last day of August she slipped her moorings and put to sea for the first time in 17 months to carry out post-refit trials and shakedown cruise. That afternoon she anchored down the coast in Mevagissey Bay. During the first two weeks of September she continued with the trials, anchoring each afternoon in Weymouth Bay, where she joined other units of the Home Fleet. It was an impressive sight to see the Navy's latest battleship, together with the older *Duke of York*, *Anson* and *Howe*, together with the aircraft carriers *Theseus*, *Vengeance* and *Victorious*. It was during this period that 100 members of the ship's company, who were due for demobilization, were given permission for their service to be extended to the summer of 1949 so that they could be onboard for the royal tour. Captain Parham said of the men, "I felt very strongly that these young men had earned the honour, as they had helped to keep the ship's heart beating during the long months in dockyard hands." On Saturday 18 September *Vanguard* left Portland and set course for Gibraltar, where she arrived three days later to carry out exercises in the western Mediterranean. However, on account of the fittings and furnishings in the royal apartments, none of which was designed to withstand the blast or shock of gunfire, Captain Parham was ordered to limit the firing of *Vanguard's* main armament to single gun salvoes with reduced charges from "A" and "B" turrets only.

On Friday 1 October *Vanguard* left Gibraltar Bay to steam east for Malta. That afternoon she passed a US Army transport with General Omar Bradley on board, and appropriate salutes were exchanged. After a passage of three days, at 1030 on Monday 4 October the battleship entered Grand Harbour for the first time to secure to No 13 buoy in Bighi Bay. During the nine days in harbour many younger members of the ship's company sampled for the first time the entertainments of Strait Street (The Gut), with its cosmopolitan mix of bars and music halls which were reminiscent of Edwardian times, providing a run ashore that was unrivalled in the Mediterranean. On 13 October, however, *Vanguard* steamed out of harbour to undertake three days of exercises in the waters off Malta, anchoring each afternoon in Marsaxlokk Bay. It was on the last day of the exercises, at 0920 on Thursday 21 October, that *Vanguard* weighed anchor to carry out gunnery practice with the forward 5.25-inch guns. Just over half an hour after leaving Marsaxlokk, and just as the firing was about to begin, there was a tragic accident when one of the ship's Royal Marines Detachment, 19-year-old Marine Edward J. Bray from Monkstown, County Dublin, was caught between the fixed and moving structures of one of the 5.25-inch gun turrets and was killed instantly as the machinery crushed him. The only time personnel could enter or leave the turret was when it was trained forward to aft. On this occasion the safety lock had not been properly engaged and the gun turret actually shifted as the unfortunate marine was entering. The tragedy was an appalling end to what had been successful trials, and as *Vanguard* returned to Grand Harbour that afternoon the atmosphere on board was somewhat subdued. The funeral service took place the next day.

On the morning of Thursday 4 November the battleship left Malta to return to Devonport, where she arrived alongside on Friday 12 November. Since leaving Devonport ten weeks earlier she had steamed 5,000 miles and had carried out an extensive programme of sea exercises and harbour drills.

Soon after her arrival in Devonport work continued with the final refurbishment and fitting out of the royal quarters. This was stopped suddenly however, when, in late November, owing to the King's illness, the royal tour to New Zealand and Australia was postponed indefinitely. On board *Vanguard* the news was broken to the ship's company by Captain Parham who told them, "As I told you on the way back from the shakedown cruise, I was supremely confident that we should have made an absolutely first class job of that mission." It was a great disappointment for *Vanguard's* ship's company, but it meant that a greater number of men would be able to spend Christmas at home.

Five days later, on Monday 29 November, it was announced that the battleship, instead of sailing to the Pacific, would be made ready for sea at the end of January as planned, and that she would join the Mediterranean Fleet where she would remain until August that year.

It was on Thursday 3 February 1949 that *Vanguard*, in company with the destroyer *Alamein*, left Devonport to set course for Gibraltar where she would take part in exercises with the cruiser *Superb* and the destroyers *Aisne*, *Alamein*, *St James*, *Solebay* and *Jutland*. On Thursday 24 February, during gunnery practice in the exercise areas off Gibraltar, the battleship's 15-inch guns of "A", "B" and "X" turrets were fired. The exercises continued into March, and during the first week of that month *Vanguard* joined a combined force from the Home and Mediterranean Fleets, which included the aircraft carrier *Triumph* and the destroyer *Volage*, for five days of exercises and manoeuvres. The C-in-C Mediterranean Fleet, Admiral Sir Arthur J. Power, hoisted his flag in *Vanguard* on 1 March. On Wednesday 16 March came the *Vanguard's* first "foreign" visit of the commission

Captain Parham, his officers and men, pose for the traditional ship's company photograph whilst the ship is in Grand Harbour Malta.

(Frank McGuinness)

For three hours during the afternoon of Tuesday 3 May 1949 *Vanguard* fired her main armament at a target on the Filfa gunnery range off Malta. In this photograph Y turret provides an awesome display of firepower. Note that the saluting platform has been replaced by the original twin 40mm Bofors mount.

(Frank McGuinness)

The fall of shot makes quite a splash around the target. Note the observation balloon overhead.

(Frank McGuinness)

A rare aerial view of the Royal Navy's last battleship firing a full 15-inch broadside.

(Joe Michie)

The singer Gracie Fields entertaining the ship's company during *Vanguard's* visit to Naples in March 1949.

(Frank McGuinness)

when she steamed into Algiers Harbour and secured stern to the jetty. On Wednesday 23 March, three days after leaving Algiers, *Vanguard* secured to a buoy in Toulon Harbour and that afternoon, in a ceremony on the ship's quarterdeck, the British Consul-General presented decorations to some 20 French men and women from the Toulon region who had rendered distinguished service to the Allied cause during the Second World War. During her stay in port the boats' crews took part in a sailing regatta, and a ship's company dance was held ashore. From Toulon *Vanguard* steamed to Naples where she moored in the harbour for a four-day visit, during which the singer Gracie Fields came across from her home on the island of Capri to entertain the ship's company from the top of one of the 15-inch gun turrets. After leaving Naples on 1 April *Vanguard* sailed south for Malta. During exercises off the island she embarked a unit of 42 Commando, Royal Marines, for transfer to Tripoli,

where she spent four days at anchor. When on the final day of the visit she was open to visitors. Only 300 British Army personnel and their families, who were from nearby bases, took advantage of the opportunity.

After leaving Tripoli *Vanguard* returned to the Malta exercise areas where, once again, her 15-inch guns were fired, this time for a bombardment of shore targets on Filfa gunnery range. Following her gunnery practice *Vanguard* took part in a convoy escort exercise with the destroyers *Chequers* and *Childers*, with the depot ship *Forth* acting as a merchant vessel. On Friday 6 May she returned to Grand Harbour. During her stay in Malta, on Sunday 15 May, the battleship was opened to the public and among those who visited the ship were the players of the First Division Football Club Chelsea, together with their Directors and Managers, who posed for a photograph with Captain Parham.

The battleship's next "foreign" visit came on Thursday 19 May when, on a very foggy day, she anchored in Venice Harbour for a five-day official stay. On Sunday 22 May Princess Margaret, who was in Venice at the time, paid a four-hour visit to the ship and attended a service in the chapel. She also contacted her father by radio from the ship and received permission for the main brace to be spliced, and for a second tot of rum to be issued. Later that month *Vanguard* visited Palermo where she joined the US Navy's aircraft carrier, *Coral Sea*. By the end of May, however, she was back in Malta's Grand Harbour and it was Monday 13 June before her summer cruise got under way once again when she sailed for Famagusta. After just four hours at anchor off the Cypriot port, during which time Admiral Power entertained the town's mayor for lunch, the battleship sailed for Port Said.

At the end of the Second World War Egypt had become a gigantic staging post for the British military forces and, despite the 1936 treaty which limited Britain to just 10,000 troops in the Suez Canal zone, the British Government was reluctant to scale numbers down. Naturally the Egyptian people did not approve of such a massive foreign military presence in their country and in 1946 and 1947 there had been some violent anti-British riots in Alexandria and Cairo. The Egyptian Prime Minister, Nakrashy Pasha, summed up his country's grievance when he declared, "The presence of foreign troops on our soil, even if stationed in a distant area, is wounding to the national dignity." Sadly for future Anglo-Egyptian relations his words were not taken too seriously by the British Government and seven years later it would be a much more forceful Egyptian leader who ensured a very

On Sunday 22 May 1949, whilst the battleship was in Venice, HRH Princess Margaret, who was in the city at the time, took the opportunity to visit *Vanguard*. Here she is inspecting the Boys' Division. *(Frank McGuinness)*

In June 1949 *Vanguard* made an official visit to Piraeus where King Paul of the Hellenes was received on board by the C-in-C Mediterranean Fleet, Admiral Sir Arthur J. Power. In this photograph the King inspects members of the ship's company.

(Frank McGuinness)

undignified removal of these "foreign" troops. Fortunately, in the summer of 1949, with all British troops having withdrawn to the canal zone, there was little civil disorder in Egypt, and the purpose of *Vanguard's* visit was to both "show the flag" and remind Egyptian leaders that Britain was still a power to be reckoned with in the Mediterranean.

After firing a 21-gun national salute *Vanguard* moored in Port Said Harbour at 0730 on Friday 17 June, and within half an hour the familiar pontoon walkway between the ship and shore was in place and leave was granted to the ship's company until midnight on each day of the ship's stay. The visit to Port Said lasted for four days, and on Sunday 19 June the battleship was opened to the public for two hours. At 0700 on 21 June, however, she slipped her moorings and under her own steam she moved slowly south to the mouth of the Suez Canal where tugs turned her so that she could steam out of harbour and back into the Mediterranean Sea. It was the closest that *Vanguard* ever came to the Red Sea and the East Indies Fleet. Once clear of Port Said the battleship set course for Beirut where, at 0815am the next day, she anchored off the city and Admiral Power was able to entertain the country's president. With the state of Israel having been set up the previous year (in contravention of United Nations resolutions for partition of Palestine

between Arabs and Jews), the political situation in the area was, as it remains today, very unstable and paramilitary organisations were active in Lebanon. In order to protect *Vanguard*, which represented a high-profile target whilst she was at anchor, the ship's divers maintained a 24-hour watch on the underwater hull, with light explosive charges being detonated at intervals. Ashore, however, the city of Beirut remained a haven for social activities and on one evening an outdoor ball was held for the ship at the American College for Middle Eastern Studies. After three days *Vanguard* left Beirut and steamed northwest to Athens where, at 0830 on Thursday 30 June, anchored in Phaleron Bay outside Piraeus. That evening Admiral Power held a formal dinner on board at which King Paul of Greece and Field Marshal Jan Smuts were guests. With the Greek Government having recently overcome a Communist uprising in the country, Admiral Power was keen to, "Show the British flag, which is a symbol of freedom." Next day King Paul returned to *Vanguard* and made a one and a half-hour tour of the ship. The visit came to an end three days later when the battleship weighed anchor and set course for Taranto, the final port of call on her summer cruise. Here she stayed for another three days. On leaving the Italian naval base *Vanguard* set course for the return passage to Malta. As she neared

HMS Vanguard leaving Malta's Grand Harbour.

(Michael Cassar)

the island Admiral Power struck his flag and transferred to the dispatch vessel *Surprise*, which marked the end of the battleship's brief period as the flagship of the Mediterranean Fleet. After a short stop at Marsaxlokk to embark a draft of UK-bound ratings, *Vanguard* sailed for Tripoli to take a small part in international diplomacy. Libya had been colonised by Italy in October 1912 when the Ottoman Empire's North African regions of Cyrenaica, Tripolitania and Fezzan were ceded following a full-scale invasion by Italian troops. One of those who resisted the Italians was the Emir of Cyrenaica, Idris al-Sannusi, who was forced to flee the country after the Italian victory. The name Libya (from the Egyptian "Lebu") was first applied to the country in 1934 when the Italians created a single administrative area for the three regions of their colony. Italy's colonial presence in Libya was ended by the Second World War, when the British Army occupied Cyrenaica and Tripolitania, while Free French forces occupied the Fezzan. In 1947 Italy renounced its colonies and Libya came under the protection of the United Nations, although Britain and France maintained administrative trusteeship. Throughout the following years the United Nations searched for a permanent solution and a proposal from Britain that she take a ten-year mandate of Cyrenaica, Italy a similar mandate over Tripolitania and France retain control of Fezzan for the same period, was heavily defeated in the General Assembly. It was clear that the best solution was complete independence for Libya, and the front runner as the first monarch for the federation was Emir Idris al-Sannusi of Cyrenaica, who had returned to the country from his exile in Egypt. In the summer of 1949, as a first step towards complete independence, Britain was negotiating with the Emir for the internal self-government of Cyrenaica and he had been invited to Britain to agree a constitution. In those days, however, with long-distance air travel being very limited and with none of the big shipping companies providing a passenger service between Tripoli and Southampton, Captain Parham was ordered to embark the Emir, his Prime Minister and their staff and convey them to Marseilles where they could take the overland route to London. After anchoring off Tripoli at 0700 on Tuesday 12 July the Emir and his considerable retinue along with large amounts of luggage were embarked, then three hours later *Vanguard* weighed anchor and set course for Marseilles. During the passage Joe Michie, one of *Vanguard's* Electrical Officers, recalled that during the passage the Emir spent most of his time sitting on the battleship's quarterdeck watching the sea and the ship's wake. Two days later *Vanguard* anchored in Marseilles Roads where the Emir and his staff were

disembarked. Shortly afterwards the battleship set course for home.

Finally, on the afternoon of Thursday 21 July she arrived back at Devonport where she secured alongside 6 & 7 wharves. Since her departure in February she had steamed some 14,350 miles. Now the ship's company were able to take a combined Easter and summer leave period.

Seven days after arriving back in her home port, on Thursday 28 July 1949, there was a change of command when, at 0940, Captain G. V. Gladstone joined the ship and later in the day Rear-Admiral Parham departed. Captain Gladstone had first gone to sea in 1917 as a midshipman in the battleship *HMS Tiger* and, like his predecessors in *Vanguard*, he was a gunnery specialist.

After a 17-day period of dry docking, *Vanguard* sailed from Devonport on 23 September and headed north for the Clyde where she carried out engine trials in the area. She eventually returned to Devonport on 6 October. Two weeks later she was given a new role when it was announced that she would take the place of *HMS Anson* as the flagship of the Home Fleet Training Squadron. The changeover started on Thursday 3 November when the *Anson* berthed astern of *Vanguard* and one week later the latter made the short six-hour passage to Portland. Two days after her arrival, on Saturday 12 November, the Flag Officer Training Squadron, Rear-Admiral E. M. Evans-Lombe, hoisted his flag in the battleship, having transferred from the aircraft carrier *Victorious*.

As part of the Home Fleet training squadron *Vanguard's* Men under Training would start their day at 0600, and at 0830 they would fall in by Divisions before going to their classrooms for instruction. At midday there was a 40-minute meal break before most of them would go ashore for sports activities. They then returned to the classrooms until 1600 when they secured for the day. On most days shore leave was granted from 1630 until 2300, with the journey to shore being made by a shuttle service of the ship's own boats. For many weeks of the year units of the training squadron would remain moored to buoys in Portland Harbour. It became a standing joke that they rested on huge piles of empty condensed milk cans. They did, however, put to sea several times each year and on these occasions they would either take part in squadron manoeuvres, or exercises with other units of the Home Fleet.

Vanguard's first major deployment as a training ship came on 28 January 1950 when, with *Victorious* and *Implacable*, she joined the Home Fleet's aircraft carrier *Vengeance* and the destroyers *Alamein* and *Gabbard* for a cruise to Gibraltar, during which a con-

An aerial view of the Royal Navy's last battleship. During 1950, as flagship of the Home Fleet Training Squadron, *Vanguard* spent a great deal of time swinging round a buoy in Portland Harbour.

(Tony Rees)

Vanguard moored in Portland Harbour with summer awnings spread over the quarterdeck.　　　　*(Tony Rees)*

voy escort exercise was undertaken. During the passage a Stoker Petty Officer who was suffering from appendicitis was transferred to *Vanguard* and on the evening of the last day of January the battleship's MO operated successfully on the sick man.

The squadron spent eight days alongside in Gibraltar before sailing on 10 February for the return passage to Portland. Three days after leaving Gibraltar, as the ships steamed through severe storms in the Bay of Biscay, at 0108 on 13 February an SOS message was received from a small French cargo ship, *SS Boffa*, whose cargo had shifted, leaving the vessel in danger of sinking. *Vanguard* immediately increased speed and for over four hours she ploughed through the mountainous seas at 20 knots to reach the scene. Finally, at 0515, with *Boffa* just 2,500 yards on the starboard bow, the battleship reduced speed and manoeuvred into a position astern of the cargo ship. Despite the 50-knot winds and high waves *Vanguard* was able to take the *Boffa* in tow, and for the next 17 hours she her pulled towards the shore and safety. In the early hours of Tuesday 14 February, however, with the weather having moderated and with her cargo redistributed, *Boffa* was out of danger and she was able to continue under her own power. At just after 0300 that morning *Vanguard* parted company with the merchant ship, and next day anchored in Weymouth Bay.

Just under three weeks later, on Monday 6 March, *Vanguard* sailed once again and this time she steamed up the Channel to Dover where, on the following day, she anchored and prepared to salute the French President, Vincent Auriol, who was making a state visit to Britain. The President and his wife crossed the Channel in the steamer *Arromanches* and half way across they were met by an escort of five Royal Navy destroyers. At midday on Tuesday 7 March, as *Arromanches* came into sight, dressed overall, *Vanguard's* ship's company manned the guard rails and a 21-gun salute was fired. As the crash of the saluting guns died away, twelve of the RAF's Vampire fighters screamed overhead, after which a silence fell as *Arromanches* steamed into Dover Harbour. During the next two days, whilst the French President and his wife were officially welcomed at various functions in London, *Vanguard* steamed up and down the Channel. At midnight on 9 March, she again anchored off Dover to salute the President upon his departure at noon on Friday 10 March. As *Arromanches* left the eastern exit of the harbour (the other entrance was still barred by sunken blockships left over from the war), M. Auriol and his wife were on deck to see *Vanguard* fire her 21-gun salute in honour of the French leader. Then, as the French ship steamed past the battleship, the destroyers *Zephyr*, *Wizard*, *Wrangler*, *Finisterre* and *Roebuck* escorted her towards Calais until French

The pride of the Royal Navy and Britain's merchant marine together in Cowes Roads on 1 August 1950. The liner *Queen Elizabeth* was outward bound from Southampton to Cherbourg and New York, while *Vanguard* was in the Solent for Cowes Week.

(*Beken of Cowes Ltd*)

naval units took over the task. Before *Vanguard* left the area, however, Captain Gladstone sent a message to the Mayor of Folkestone telling him that during the afternoon he would bring *Vanguard* very close to the town enabling onlookers, and particularly school-children, to obtain a good view of the battleship. In the event thousands of people were able to watch the warship as she steamed past on her way back to Portland. By the morning of Saturday 11 March she was once again swinging round A6 buoy in Portland Harbour.

As *Vanguard* lay at her Portland mooring during the spring of 1950, the outgoing C-in-C of the US Navy's Atlantic Fleet, Admiral H. P. Blandy, publicly and very bluntly declared in the United States that the battleship in its original role as a major fighting unit on the high seas was, "as dead as the dodo." He went on to say that, "There is therefore no use in keeping battleships in commission, unless it is as training ships." It was confirmation of what the powers that be in the Admiralty already appreciated, and it would only be a matter of weeks before *Vanguard* was the only battleship left in full commission in the Royal Navy. It was clear to most informed observers that her career would not continue much longer, and it was difficult to envisage any useful operational role for her.

In June 1950 *Vanguard* spent a long weekend at Torquay where she was again opened to the public. In July she spent a few days in Bangor Bay for a short visit to Northern Ireland. Later that month she anchored in Cowes Roads in the Solent for the Royal Yacht Squadron's Regatta, Cowes Week. But by the end of the first week in August she was back at Portland. On Friday 18 August, Captain D. H. Hall-Thompson arrived on board at 0930 to relieve Captain Gladstone who left the ship that afternoon to take up his new appointment as Commodore of the Royal Naval Barracks, Chatham. Early the next month, on 7 September, with *Vanguard* having steamed to Portsmouth, Rear-Admiral Evans-Lombe struck his flag. Just six days later, Admiral Sir Philip Vian hoisted his flag in the battleship, so that she became once again the Home Fleet's flagship. Next day, after embarking the First Lord of the Admiralty, Lord Hall, who was taking passage to Gibraltar and spending a week with the fleet, *Vanguard* left Portsmouth to rendezvous with the aircraft carrier *Vengeance* (Flag Rear-Admiral C. E. Lambe, FO 3rd Aircraft Carrier Squadron), the cruisers *Cleopatra* and *Swiftsure* of the 2nd Cruiser Squadron and 11 destroyers as they set course for the Home Fleet's autumn cruise. Among the destroyers were *Agincourt, Corunna, Crossbow, Gabbard, Reward, St Kitts, Solebay* and *Sluys*.

The fleet arrived in Gibraltar on 20 September where they remained for three weeks. They were joined by a Canadian Squadron consisting of the aircraft carrier *Magnificent* and the destroyers *Micmac* and *Huron*, under Rear-Admiral E. R. Mainguy RCN. Whilst at Gibraltar the Home Fleet was joined by units of the Mediterranean Fleet which made an impressive display of naval power with over 20 warships in port. The combined fleet exercises began on 12 October, and during the manoeuvres aircraft from the two carriers, which were operating well out of the battleship's range, once again highlighted the capital ship's vulnerability to air attack when they made dummy bombing and torpedo runs over *Vanguard*. Soon afterwards *Vanguard's* ship's company got their first "foreign" run ashore with a five-day visit to St Vincent in the Cape Verde Islands. This was followed on Friday 27 October by a five-day visit to Madeira, where the battleship anchored in the picturesque Funchal Bay, just a few hundred yards from the town's pier. After leaving Madeira *Vanguard* returned to Gibraltar where, on 24 November, the Royal Marines Detachment provided a Guard of Honour at Government House during a visit to the colony by the Duke of Edinburgh. The final port of call during the cruise was Lisbon, on Wednesday 29 November, when the battleship negotiated the River Tagus to berth alongside in the docks for a six-day visit to the city. After leaving the Tagus on the morning of Monday 4 December, the battleship rendezvoused with the destroyers *Battleaxe, St Kitts* and *Solebay*, for the return passage to Portsmouth, where she arrived alongside South Railway Jetty on Thursday 7 December. Five days later the ship received a visit from Winston Churchill who, with his wife, was in Portsmouth to receive the Freedom of the City. Whilst Mrs Churchill paid a visit to *HMS Indomitable*, the aircraft carrier she had launched in March 1940, her husband made a fleeting half-hour call on *Vanguard* where he addressed the ship's company on the quarterdeck. A week later Admiral Vian transferred his flag to the *Indomitable*.

With the ship's company having taken their seasonal leave, the *Vanguard* left Portsmouth again for Gibraltar on 19 January 1951. Three days later she secured alongside the colony's south mole to await other units of the Home Fleet for joint anti-submarine exercises with the US Navy's Sixth Fleet. On Saturday 10 February *Indomitable*, with Admiral Vian on board, arrived in Gibraltar. At 1625, as the carrier was manoeuvring alongside, a sudden squall blew up and she collided with Vanguard's stern. Fortunately damage was not too serious, and the hole in the battleship's stern was filled with concrete and painted grey. The collision did not prevent either ship from sailing two days later for the exercises, with *Vanguard* once again flying the C-in-C's flag. During

Flying the flag of the C-in-C Home Fleet, Admiral Sir Philip Vian, *Vanguard* leaves Portsmouth Harbour on 19 January 1951 bound for Gibraltar.   *(Tony Rees)*

the manoeuvres aircraft from *Indomitable* made a mock attack on *Vanguard*, resulting in the battleship being declared "sunk". This was yet another reminder of the battleship's obsolescence in the post-war world. On completion of the manoeuvres the units of the Home Fleet began a series of visits to Italian ports along the Ligurian coast, with the cruiser *Swiftsure* visiting the beautiful resort of San Remo, the Sixth Frigate Flotilla visiting Savona and *Vanguard* going alongside in Genoa. For the battleship this was followed by six days anchored at Villefranche. By Wednesday 14 March Admiral Vian had struck his flag and she was back in Devonport for a seven-week maintenance period, which included four weeks in No 10 dry dock.

It was in early May 1951 before *Vanguard* put to sea again. On the morning of Tuesday 8 May she anchored off Dover once more to salute a visiting Head of State. This time she was in position to welcome King Frederick IX and Queen Ingrid of Denmark who arrived aboard the Danish royal yacht, *Kronprinsesse Ingrid*. At noon she steamed past *Vanguard* as the battleship's complement manned ship and a 21-gun salute was fired. Clearly the King was impressed by this welcome for he sent a congratulatory signal to Captain Hall-Thompson on the smart

appearance of *Vanguard* and her ship's company. Later that afternoon the battleship returned to the Training Squadron at Portland after an absence of eight months. She hoisted the flag of Rear-Admiral R. M. Dick, the Flag Officer Training Squadron, and took part in Navy Days. That summer she made a number of visits to south coast resorts, including Bournemouth and Eastbourne to "show the flag," and took part in "Shop Window" exercises off the Isle of Wight when, for the second time in her career a helicopter landed on her quarterdeck.

In early July, in company with the aircraft carriers *Indomitable* and *Indefatigable*, she steamed north to Scapa Flow, anchoring there on 4 July. Over the next eight days the Training Squadron's sailing regatta was held in foggy conditions. When *Vanguard* left the anchorage on 12 July it was to steam south to Portland, where she arrived three days later.

The remainder of the summer was spent swinging round A6 buoy again at Portland. In the second week of September Rear-Admiral Dick transferred his flag to *Indefatigable*. A few days later, on 16 September, *Vanguard* left the Training Squadron to make the short passage to Devonport where, the following day, she started a five-month refit, after which she was to become the flagship of the Home Fleet.

During *Vanguard's* visit to Villefranche in February 1951 a Dragonfly helicopter from the aircraft carrier *Indomitable* landed on the battleship's forecastle. There were virtually no safety measures taken for this dangerous manoeuvre.

(Imperial War Museum A31846)

This view from *Indomitable* on 1 July 1951 shows *Vanguard* and *Indefatigable* en route to Scapa Flow.

(Frederick Presswell)

Chapter Five

Flagship of the Home and Reserve Fleets
November 1951 to December 1960

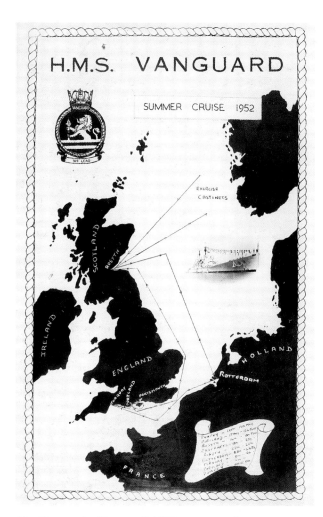

H.M.S. VANGUARD

SUMMER CRUISE 1952

The itinerary for *Vanguard's* 1952 summer cruise.

(D. G. Collins)

In late November 1951, as *Vanguard* lay in Devonport Dockyard's No 10 dry dock undergoing her first major refit, it was announced from Buckingham Palace that the King, who was recovering from an operation for lung cancer, "hoped to be able to take a sea voyage lasting some weeks in the early spring." It was also made clear that this would be on board *Vanguard* which would not now become the Home Fleet's flagship until the cruise was over.

Before this however, there was a change of command when on Friday 21 December 1951, Captain J. S. S. Litchfield OBE RN took over from Captain Hall-Thompson, who left the ship that morning.

By the New Year of 1952 *Vanguard's* refit was nearing completion and on 11 January the King's Equerry, Group Captain Peter Townsend, and the Deputy Master of the Household, visited the ship to assist with arrangements for the fitting out of the royal apartments for the proposed cruise. Two weeks later the battleship was shifted from the dry dock to the sea wall at 5 & 6 wharves, where everything seemed to be proceeding according to schedule. Suddenly, however, at 1145 on Wednesday 6 February 1952, news was received that King George VI had died at Sandringham in the early hours of the morning, and later in the day Captain Litchfield addressed the ship's company. Next day, the battleship's engineers carried out basin trials after which a detachment from the ship's company, who had been rapidly selected to take part in the King's funeral procession, started practising for the occasion. With the funeral ceremony having taken place on 15 February, *Vanguard* left Devonport Dockyard a week later to carry out her planned post-refit trials off Gibraltar.

During the passage south there were again reminders of the vulnerability of battleships when torpedo-carrying aircraft from *Indomitable* made mock attacks on *Vanguard* and several "hits" were recorded. During her trials in the western Mediterranean *Vanguard* carried out manoeuvres with *Indomitable* and the training squadron's carrier, *Implacable* and the fast minelayer *Apollo*, but on 26 March, together with *Indomitable*, she sailed for home and arrived at Spithead three days later. Next day, Monday 31 March, she moved up harbour and secured alongside South Railway Jetty. During the Easter holiday of 1952 *Vanguard* took part in Portsmouth's Navy Days, and on the three afternoons when she was opened to the public she attracted almost 30,000 visitors. Although as a fighting ship she was obsolete, there is no doubt that she still captured the public imagination as no other type of warship could. By this time *Vanguard* was the Royal Navy's only operational battleship and the public clearly wanted to see her. On

HMS Vanguard at anchor in Plymouth Sound.   *(Tony Rees)*

Vanguard steams up Holland's New Waterway in June 1952 for an official visit to Rotterdam.   *(Tony Rees)*

Tuesday 13 May 1952, *Vanguard* once again became the flagship of the Home Fleet when the C-in-C, Admiral Sir G. E. Creasy, transferred from *Indomitable* and hoisted his flag onboard. Three days later *Vanguard* left for Portland, and in the second week of June she steamed north to Rosyth where she met *Eagle* and the Dutch aircraft carrier *Karel Doorman* (and other ships) to take part in "Exercise Castanets", which was designed to test the Home Fleet's air defences. At the end of the exercise, in company with the destroyers *Battleaxe* and *Broadsword*, *Vanguard* set course down the North Sea for an official visit to Rotterdam, where she arrived on the morning of Saturday 28 June. During the evening of 1 July Admiral Creasy welcomed Queen Juliana and Prince Bernhard to a reception on board, and during the evening the royal guests made a boat trip in the vicinity of the battleship to view the magnificent floodlighting. On the following day the ship's compa-

ny held a children's party on board, and on the last day of the visit, with the ship opened to the public, over 10,000 people came to look round. After leaving Rotterdam and carrying out a full-power trial in the Channel, *Vanguard* spent three days at anchor in Torbay before carrying out gunnery practice off the Isle of Wight. She finally entered Portsmouth Harbour and secured alongside South Railway Jetty on 10 July.

It was on Friday 22 August 1952 that *Vanguard* left Portsmouth with *Apollo* to steam north to Invergordon, where she spent the remainder of the month at anchor. She put to sea for the first two days of September then on the morning of Sunday 7 September, together with the destroyer *Battleaxe*, she left the area to steam through the Pentland Firth to Greenock where a NATO fleet was assembling for a major exercise code-named "Main Brace". As well as *Vanguard* other major Royal Navy units taking part included the aircraft carriers *Eagle* and *Illustrious*, the

Refuelling from an RFA during "Exercise Main Brace". *(Imperial War Museum A32283)*

In November 1952 *Vanguard* and other units steamed north to Arctic waters to give the ship's company some experience of operating in severe weather conditions. In this view she steams close to Jan Mayen Island. *(D. G. Collins)*

An icebound forecastle and forward 15-inch guns... *(D. G. Collins)*

...And enough snow to build a snowman. *(D. G. Collins)*

cruiser *Swiftsure* and the destroyers *Aisne*, *Battleaxe* and *Ulster*. From the US Navy came the aircraft carriers *Wasp*, *Wright* and the *Franklin D. Roosevelt*, as well as the battleship *Wisconsin* and the cruiser *Columbus*. The exercise, which was under the overall command of the US Navy's Admiral McCormick, NATO's Supreme Allied Commander, Atlantic, started on Saturday 13 September when the powerful concentration of warships left the Clyde for northern waters. The exercise was in two phases which were designed to show Allied plans for air and sea support for Norway and Denmark in case of war, and to reassure the Scandinavian countries that they were not being ignored by NATO. The whole force steamed north into Arctic waters where the already poor weather conditions deteriorated still further, resulting in heavy seas and storm force winds. Although the severe weather disrupted the carriers' flying programmes, they still provided the force's main offensive power and the two battleships, *Vanguard* and *Wisconsin*, more or less tagged along. They did, however, provide some support when 1,500 US Marines were landed on the Jutland peninsular. It was yet another reminder that the battleship had been superseded by the aircraft carrier.

"Exercise Main Brace" was completed on Tuesday 23 September, and three days later *Vanguard* joined the rest of the fleet at Oslo, where the various debriefings were being held. During the battleship's six days at anchor she received visits from Crown Prince Olav and Prince Harold of Norway. She left on 2 October to carry out exercises with *Eagle*, during which the carrier's Fireflies "attacked" the battleship. These manoeuvres ended on the afternoon of 4 October when both the *Eagle* and *Vanguard* anchored at Rosyth where the latter received a visit from her former commanding officer, Rear-Admiral Gladstone. Five days later the battleship sailed north for Invergordon where she spent the remainder of October, with only one day at sea for gunnery practice. The first 12 days of November were spent in and around Invergordon, before the battleship moved south to Rosyth where she rendezvoused with *Eagle* and the destroyers *Agincourt*, *Aisne*, *Corunna*, *Diamond*, *Venus*, *Verulam* and *Virago* for a cruise to Arctic waters. The purpose of "the cruise" was to give officers and ratings some experience of operations in severe weather conditions, and to test equipment and communications. The ships would carry out fleet manoeuvres and anti-submarine exercises, during which carrier-borne and shore-based aircraft would "attack" the force. After leaving Rosyth on Monday 17 November the ships steamed to an area in the Greenland Sea, west of the Greenwich meridian and close to Jan Mayen Island where, for several days, the ships' companies operated their vessels in the Arctic darkness and in temperatures of 30 degrees below zero. At 1250 on Thursday 20 November, when *Vanguard* was just a few miles from Jan Mayen Island, she was "attacked" by four of *Eagle's* Attacker jet fighters, and later that day the guns' crews closed up for 5.25-inch gunnery firing. During the manoeuvres *Vanguard* made radio contact with a British expedition to North Greenland which lay 20 feet under the snow! The exercises continued as the fleet moved south. By 25 November they were in warmer waters off the island of Guernsey, and on Monday 1 December *Vanguard* returned to Portsmouth to allow for Christmas and New Year leave. On Christmas Day *Vanguard* was visited by carol singers from *Indomitable*. On Monday 19 January 1953 there was a change of command when Captain R. A. Ewing DSC RN took over from Captain Litchfield. Next day *Vanguard* left Portsmouth in thick fog and set course for Gibraltar where she was to be dry docked. As she steamed round the Isle of Wight the fog which had surrounded her all the way through Spithead cleared and bright sunlight broke through to herald her first

cruise of the year. She arrived alongside the colony's south mole on Saturday 24 January and four days later, with the aid of tugs, she was moved into the No 1 dry dock. She was the biggest ship to have used the dry dock and the operation required great skill as there was only eight feet of clearance at either side of the hull. The maintenance period lasted for five weeks until Monday 2 March when, having embarked the First Sea Lord, she sailed for a series of exercises with the aircraft carriers *Eagle*, *Indomitable* and *Theseus*, the cruisers *Glasgow* and *Bermuda*, and the destroyers *Diamond* and *Venus*. During the manoeuvres *Eagle* lost an Attacker and two Sea Hornet aircraft, and by 5 March the battleship was back alongside Gibraltar's south mole. On Tuesday 17 March *Vanguard* left Gibraltar once again and after more exercises with *Eagle* and *Indomitable* she left the area and steamed north for a long weekend visit to Brest before returning to Portsmouth, where she arrived on the morning of Wednesday 25 March.

After taking part in Portsmouth's Navy Days over the first weekend in April, during which almost 31,000 people visited the ship, *Vanguard* moved to Portland on Friday 8 May. She remained there for

An iced-up *Vanguard* and the destroyer *Corunna* carry out a jackstay transfer north of the Arctic Circle.

(D. G. Collins)

Ice and snow cover the anchor cables... *(D. G. Collins)*

...And the guard rails. *(D. G. Collins)*

Vanguard is manoeuvred into Gibraltar's No 1 dry dock for her annual overhaul.

Framed by the dockyard crane the battleship is settled into the dry dock.   *(MoD/Crown Copyright)*

A fine shot of *Vanguard* leaving Portsmouth in May 1953.   *(Tony Rees)*

almost three weeks until 28 May when she left for an official visit to Southend. Next day, at 1000, the battleship arrived off the Kentish Knock light vessel and that afternoon anchored in the Thames Estuary, off Southend Pier, where shore leave was immediately granted.

At 0050 on the morning of Saturday 30 May, however, when *MFV 1124* was returning liberty men to the ship from ashore, a Stoker fell overboard and, despite a long search, his body could not be found. Next day there was a minor drama when one of the ship's launches was called out to rescue a broken down pleasure boat which was full of visitors bound for *Vanguard*.

The battleship left Southend on Friday 5 June to return to Portland, but in the early hours of 9 June, three days after her arrival, she sailed once again, this time to rendezvous with the aircraft carriers *Eagle*, *Indomitable*, *Indefatigable* and *Implacable*, after which all five capital ships steamed to their Spithead anchorages to prepare for the Queen's Coronation Review of the Fleet. As the Home Fleet's flagship the *Vanguard* took the "plum" anchorage at the head of F line, alongside *Eagle*. It was the last time that a bat-

tleship would take part in a fleet review. By Friday 12 June all the British, Commonwealth and foreign warships had assembled at Spithead for the Review itself. Two days later, on Sunday 14 June, the Queen embarked in *HMS Surprise* and next day at 3pm, preceded by the Trinity House vessel *Patricia*, *Surprise* left South Railway Jetty for Spithead. Half an hour later she passed between *Vanguard* and the US Navy's heavy cruiser, *USS Baltimore*, as ships' companies manned and cheered ship.

That evening, following the Review, all the warships were illuminated and the Queen held a banquet on board the battleship which she had launched eight and a half years earlier.

With the Coronation Review over *Vanguard* left Spithead during the afternoon of Tuesday 16 June and steamed down Channel at full power, to anchor off the town of Portrush in Northern Ireland for a long weekend before steaming back to Portsmouth. She arrived on Wednesday 24 June to prepare for the embarkation of Sir Winston Churchill. The Prime Minister was scheduled to meet the US President, Dwight D. Eisenhower, for political talks about joint policies on Germany and Korea, but shortly before he was due to

The battleship anchored at Spithead on 15 June 1953.

(Maritime Photo Library)

79

In June 1953, as flagship of the Home Fleet, *Vanguard* lies anchored at Spithead for the Queen's Coronation Review of the Fleet.
(FotoFlite)

The battleship anchored at Spithead on 15 June 1953.

(FotoFlite)

Dressed overall for the Fleet Review, *Vanguard* makes a splendid sight.   *(FotoFlite)*

embark it was announced that for health reasons the Prime Minister had been forced to postpone the talks. With her transatlantic voyage having been cancelled *Vanguard* continued her summer cruise which had been planned before the arrangements for the political conference were known. She left Portsmouth on the last day of June to visit Oban, Loch Ewe and Falmouth. At the latter port, where she arrived on 15 July, she put on an evening fireworks display and again opened to visitors. 6,500 people took the opportunity to look over her, despite the long boat journey involved. By 21 July, however, *Vanguard* was back in Portsmouth and once again, during the four Navy Days, she attracted 48,175 people, far surpassing any other single ship which took part in the event. Despite this popularity with the general public, in Parliament

there was grumbling from members on both sides of the House about the cost of keeping *Vanguard* in commission.

It was in early September 1953 when *Vanguard* put to sea once again, steaming north to Invergordon. In mid-September she rendezvoused with *Eagle*, the cruiser *Swiftsure* and other ships including the battleship *USS Iowa*, for the NATO exercise "Mariner", which took place in severe weather in the Denmark Strait. During the exercise *Vanguard*, together with the destroyer *Corunna*, steamed to Latitude 75° North, some 900 miles north of John O'Groats. Icebergs became a regular feature of the surrounding seascape. The exercise ended on Saturday 3 October when *Vanguard* anchored at Greenock. Six days later she returned to Invergordon, where she remained until 21

At the conclusion of the Review all the major units left Spithead and returned to their normal duties. *Vanguard* remained at Spithead until the afternoon of 16 June. In this shot the battleship is preparing to leave as the aircraft carrier *Illustrious* steams past towards the Nab Channel.
(FotoFlite)

In September 1953 *Vanguard* took part in "Exercise Mariner" in the Denmark Strait, which saw some severe weather. In this photograph the cruiser *Sheffield* provides a screen for the battleship.

(Imperial War Museum A32751)

During "Exercise Mariner", as well as a "hostile" force, there were also some dangerous natural hazards to avoid.

(Imperial War Museum A32747)

October when she sailed south to Portland. This time the battleship spent only two days at the anchorage before, on Monday 26 October, she steamed the short distance to Portsmouth where she was to undergo a two-month maintenance period.

On Tuesday 5 January 1954, with *Vanguard* lying alongside Portsmouth's Middle Slip Jetty, Admiral Sir Michael Denny took over from Admiral Creasy as the C-in-C, Home Fleet, and hoisted his flag in the battleship. A few days later Vice-Admiral Parham, another of *Vanguard's* former commanding officers, paid a five-hour visit to his old ship, and on Thursday 21 January, flying the flag of Admiral Denny, *Vanguard* left Portsmouth for her annual docking period which, like the previous year, was to be carried out in Gibraltar. It was on Wednesday 10 March that the battleship was moved back to the south mole from the dry dock. That same day other units of the Home Fleet, including the aircraft carrier *Eagle*, arrived in Gibraltar to take part in exercises which started in the western Mediterranean on Monday 15 March. Once at sea *Vanguard* rendezvoused with the cruisers *Bermuda* and *Superb*, and destroyers to carry out convoy escort exercises. After returning to Gibraltar on

Friday 19 March she remained alongside for nine days. When she returned to sea *Vanguard* remained in the western Mediterranean for "Exercise Medflex A" along with French and Dutch naval vessels. Once again *Eagle*, *Superb* and *Bermuda* took part, as well as *Indefatigable* and the Dutch *Karel Doorman*, and British, French and Dutch destroyers. As well as air defence measures, the fleet practised dealing with the aftermath of a nuclear explosion as they steamed back towards home waters. On 1 April, *Vanguard* arrived in Portland for Customs clearance before arriving at Portsmouth Harbour the following day.

During her stay in Portsmouth it was announced that *Vanguard* would undergo a refit at Devonport in October that year, and while she was in dock Admiral Denny would shift his flag to the depot ship *Tyne*. The announcement led to rumours that the battleship was to be withdrawn from active service, but they were denied by a Government minister who said that there were no plans for *Vanguard* to be laid up. The rumours did nothing to diminish the public interest in the battleship and during Navy Days she attracted over 34,000 people during the three afternoons she was open to the public. It was during the afternoon of

Vanguard alongside at Gibraltar in March 1954. Ahead of her is the submarine depot ship *Maidstone*.

(Norman Curnow)

Major units of the Home and Mediterranean Fleets at Gibraltar in March 1954. Alongside the South Mole are *Vanguard*, *Eagle* and *Implacable*, and secured outboard of the battleship are two *Daring*-class destroyers. *(Norman Curnow)*

Friday 7 May that *Vanguard* sailed from Portsmouth to carry out air defence exercises with Avenger aircraft from RNAS Ford. She then set course for Torbay, where she anchored off the fishing port and seaside resort of Brixham. She sailed again on Wednesday 12 May to rehearse for her last "royal" engagement, which had been code-named "Operation Loyalty". In the evening she returned to Brixham and next day, at just before midnight, she sailed to rendezvous with the aircraft carrier *Triumph*, the cruiser *Glasgow* and the destroyers *Barfleur* and *Saintes*. At 0800 all the ships were dressed with masthead flags and exactly an hour later they met the brand new royal yacht, *Britannia*, which was bringing the Queen and Duke of Edinburgh home from Malta at the end of their Commonwealth Tour which had started in November 1953. After firing a 21-gun salute *Vanguard* led the escorting ships down *Britannia's* starboard side as six Sunderland and Shackleton aircraft of RAF Coastal Command flew overhead. At 1600, off Portland, the two aircraft carriers of the training squadron, *Implacable* and *Indefatigable*, joined the squadron and steamed past the Royal Yacht. Then, off the Isle of Wight, it was *Vanguard's* turn to steam past again and, for the last time, the ship's company manned ship and cheered the Queen, before the battleship set course for a weekend visit to the French port of Brest.

After leaving port *Vanguard* returned to Portland where she anchored overnight before, on the morning of 20 May, she steamed north to Rosyth where she remained until the end of the month. After putting to sea on Monday 31 May she rendezvoused with other units of the Home Fleet, including *Apollo, Duchess, Venus, Verulam* and *Vigilant*, for a series of anti-aircraft exercises. They took her to Invergordon, Loch Eriboll and Scapa Flow, the anchorage which had been so familiar to all her predecessors. During the exercises the force was "attacked" by Sea Hawk aircraft and, once again, the battleship was declared to be "sunk". At Scapa Flow *Vanguard* was opened to the public for three hours and, despite the isolated location, 400 people visited her. After leaving Scapa *Vanguard* set course for Oslo where Admiral Denny attended a NATO conference. After seven days in the Norwegian capital she steamed the short distance down the Skagerrak to anchor off Kristiansand, where she remained until Monday 5 July. She then set course for what was to be her final foreign visit, to the Swedish city of Helsingborg, where she anchored the following morning. At 1000 on Sunday 11 July she received her last royal visit when King Gustav of Sweden arrived on board to inspect the Royal Marines Guard of Honour and to spend an hour and a half with the C-in-C. It was on Monday 12 July that *Vanguard*

left Helsingborg to steam to Portland and by 21 July she was once again alongside Portsmouth's South Railway Jetty. Three days later there was a final change of command when Captain Sir John Tyrwhitt RN succeeded Captain Ewing, who had been promoted to Rear-Admiral.

That summer, during Navy Days, *Vanguard* proved to be as popular as ever when 39,520 people visited her. Perhaps many sensed that this might be their last opportunity to walk around an operational battleship. On 15 September 1954 Admiral Denny struck his flag and left *Vanguard*. Ten days later, on 25 September, the battleship left Portsmouth for the last time under her own steam and set course for Devonport. During the passage she carried out anti-submarine exercises with the submarines *Scorcher* and *Subtle*, and arrived alongside Devonport's 6 & 7 wharves at 1345 the next day. It was to be the end of *Vanguard's* active career. No sooner had she secured alongside at Devonport to start a £220,000 refit than many of her ship's company left the ship on draft and at 1145 on Friday 1 October, after handing over command to his Executive Officer, Commander H. G. Barnard RN, Captain Tyrwhitt left the ship.

In December 1954 *Vanguard* was towed into No 10 dry dock where work could be carried out to her stern glands which, it had been reported, would delay the completion of the refit. In the New Year of 1955 it was announced that the battleship would be back in service for the Home Fleet's spring manoeuvres.

In March 1955, however, came the news that *Vanguard* would recommission with a very reduced complement. Then, in a sudden reversal of policy came the announcement, which was no surprise to anyone that, on completion of her refit at the end of 1955, *Vanguard* would be placed in reserve and that many from her ship's company would be drafted to the guided missile trials ship, *Girdle Ness*.

Although she was in reserve *Vanguard* kept a small ship's company, many of whom were National Servicemen, and men under training. In early February 1956, Keith Wilkinson who, as a schoolboy, had conscientiously collected newspapers as a contribution to the cost of building *Vanguard*, was one of a number of men under training who transferred from the training carrier, *Ocean*, to the battleship which was lying in the River Tamar. He recalls that on board the carrier there had been an efficient laundry service, but in *Vanguard* there was no such luxury and he soon became proficient at doing all his washing, from underwear to boiler suits, in a zinc bucket. He also remembers keeping watch in the boiler rooms and on the auxiliary machinery, watched over by senior mechanicians. On Sunday mornings Ceremonial

HMS Vanguard under way in 1953. *(Author's collection)*

After a period under refit and in Reserve at Devonport, *Vanguard* was towed to Portsmouth where she was to become the flagship of the Reserve Fleet. *(Author's collection)*

In the late 1950s *Vanguard* became a familiar sight in Portsmouth Harbour's Fareham Creek. Moored close by her is the aircraft carrier *Theseus*. *(FotoFlite)*

Divisions were held on the quarter deck, whatever the weather, where they were inspected by the Commanding Officer. When Keith left the ship three months later and took his place in the boat to go ashore for the last time he felt he was saying "farewell to an old and trusted friend."

During 1956 there were continual rumours that she would be recommissioned. That these were not realistic was demonstrated when one Member of Parliament wrote in a newspaper: "Good it is to see the last of the Duke of York class - bad ships even among white elephants. But may all those who pay taxes or vote money to the Navy resist the survival of that paralytic mastodon, the *Vanguard*. To convert her to post-Dardanelles weapons will be, by all accounts, prohibitive, and she will swallow up men like a Moloch - men who do not exist." In October 1956, however, just a few weeks before the Suez Crisis, it was announced that in the following month *Vanguard*, would become the flagship of the Reserve Fleet as an accommodation and training ship at Portsmouth. On 26 October she was towed from Devonport to Fareham Creek in Portsmouth Harbour. On 28 November Vice-Admiral R. G. Onslow, the Flag Officer Commanding Reserve Fleet, hoisted his flag on board and Captain A. G. Poe DSC RN was appointed the Senior Officer Reserve Fleet. However, the fact that she had not been sent to the scrapyard continued to fuel controversy. This often surfaced at the time Parliament debated the Navy Estimates. In July 1958 the Parliamentary Secretary to the Admiralty reported that the battleship was being brought to a "lower state of readiness," but he went on to say that she would still be used as the Reserve Fleet Headquarters. However, in view of the fact that it was costing some £230,000 a year to maintain the battleship, in the following month a Parliamentary Select Committee recommended that, "If no positive function can be found for *Vanguard* she should be disposed of." Although the Admiralty rejected the recommendation it was clear that the political pressure to get rid of *Vanguard* could not be ignored indefinitely.

Many of the battleship's training staff transferred from the cruiser *Cleopatra* which, until relieved by *Vanguard*, had been the Reserve Fleet Flagship. Many men under training learnt their basic seamanship skills on board the battleship, and many will still have memories of pulling cutters and whalers up and around Fareham Creek on cold misty mornings as they navigated their way round the warships which were laid up awaiting disposal. Many members of the ship's company at the time will remember the usual afternoon rush to catch the boats to take them ashore at the end of each working day.

In the spring of 1957 there was a short respite when, on 1 May, six tugs towed *Vanguard* to Middle Slip Jetty, where she remained undergoing maintenance until mid-June. For most of the time, however, the battleship remained moored in Fareham Creek and the ship's company christened her "Britain's Mightiest Mothball". It was during this period that *Vanguard* was used for filming scenes from "Sink the Bismarck". William Flynn, who was an Officer's Cook onboard at the time, remembers the event: "Commander Brookes announced that we should disregard any orders in German which were broadcast over the ship's tannoy. On one occasion I saluted a 'four-ringed Captain' on the quarterdeck, only to be told by the Master at Arms that I should not salute actors. When I told him I couldn't tell the difference he replied, 'The ones wearing make up are the actors.' One day, when I was on my way to the wardroom galley I went rushing into a 'German' naval officer lying spreadeagled on the deck, with his uniform covered in what looked like blood. Suddenly, from behind me came the shout, 'Cut!' and the director told me to get off his film set."

During Navy Days in August 1959 *Vanguard* was towed alongside South Railway Jetty where, dressed overall for the occasion, with the destroyer *Scorpion* outboard, she made her final public appearance and, as always, she was very popular with the public. The end for *Vanguard* was announced a few weeks later in October 1959 when, at an Admiralty Press conference, the media were told that the battleship was to be scrapped the following year. That same day, Friday 9 October, Captain Norman Fisher, the Senior Officer Reserve Fleet, broke the news to his ship's company that *Vanguard* was to be ready for disposal by the summer of 1960. William Flynn remembers that about two months before she was finally decommissioned Rear-Admiral Grant held a gala banquet on board, at which the First Sea Lord, Admiral of the Fleet Lord Mountbatten, the C-in-C Portsmouth, Admiral Sir Manley Power and Lt-Colonel Sir Vivian Dunn, the Royal Marines Director of Music, were just a few of the VIP guests. "The sailmakers erected huge awnings on the quarterdeck and the old ship was decorated with bunting and coloured lights, she looked a splendid sight. We in the galley spent long hours preparing roast barons of beef, saddles of lamb, game birds and savouries. In the bakery the staff made lots of bread rolls, cakes, meringues and trifles, it was a magnificent spread. The banquet went on into the early hours and, although I say it myself, we wardroom cooks did a magnificent job."

On Tuesday 7 June 1960, in a simple sunset ceremony on *Vanguard's* quarterdeck, the White Ensign

HMS Vanguard's last official public appearance was for Navy Days at the end of August 1959. Here she is alongside South Railway Jetty and dressed overall. Alongside her is the destroyer *Scorpion*. Although it may have appeared to be just like the good old days, the battleship's days were numbered.

(J. M. Cox)

was lowered for the last time, watched over by Rear-Admiral Grant, who said of the occasion, "The last sunset of any ship is inevitably a sad occasion and this one more so because it marks the passing of a type of ship. The battleship is out of date and has now been replaced as a capital ship of the fleet by the aircraft carrier." He then added a final comment, which clearly ruled out any ideas of preserving *Vanguard*: "It would have been nice to preserve a modern battleship, rather as the *Victory* has been preserved, but it would be much too costly." He then transferred his flag to his new headquarters ship for the Reserve Fleet - *Sheffield*. *Vanguard* had become a dead ship. In her farewell message to *Vanguard* the Queen sent the following signal; "I have very special memories of your great ship. I launched her myself and then made my first visit to a part of the Commonwealth in her. I shall, therefore, be sharing in the feelings of you all as you lower the ensign for the last time."

Vanguard had been sold to the British Iron and Steel Corporation, part of the nationalized steel industry, for £560,000. She was to be broken up at their Faslane yard, one condition of the sale being that she should not leave the United Kingdom. Her 44,500 tons of metal were expected to fetch well over £600,000. Her final voyage was scheduled to start on the morning of Thursday 4 August 1960 when tugs would tow her out of Portsmouth Harbour for the five-day voyage to the shipbreaking yard at Faslane, in the Gareloch, just a few miles from where she had first set sail in May 1946. On board the battleship there would be a party of two officers and 60 ratings, under the command of Lt-Cdr W. G. Frampton RN, an experienced officer who had been in the Navy for 33 years, having joined in 1927 when battleships still reigned supreme.

When the day came there was no special ceremony, although all the ships in the harbour were dressed overall - but that was in honour of the Queen Mother's birthday. Five dockyard tugs shepherded *Vanguard* down harbour amid a silence which was surprising for an occasion of such significance to the Navy. Ratings

Still looking spick and span, *Vanguard* in the Reserve Fleet trot at Portsmouth. *(Maritime Photo Library)*

on other naval vessels leaned casually on the guard rails of their ships as the battleship passed by, but there were no waves or cheers, just silent curiosity as *Vanguard* slid towards the harbour mouth. The only acknowledgement came when she reached the training ship *Foudroyant*, where the boys fell in smartly and gave three cheers as the battleship came by. Perhaps it was this unexpected tribute which unsettled *Vanguard*, for as she was slowly towed towards the harbour entrance things started to go wrong - badly wrong.

Naval book publisher Mike Critchley remembers as a schoolboy he made sure he saw *Vanguard* leave harbour. He remembers "I paid my fare to cross the harbour in good time and made one or two trips across the narrow entrance on the old car ferry which pulled itself across the harbour on sturdy chains between Gosport and Point at Old Portsmouth. It was my normal route to school so I knew the route and best vantage point. After a couple of trips across harbour all boat traffic was stopped in the harbour and the ferry came to rest a few hundred yards from the Gosport shore. Definitely the best and closest vantage point for an enthusiastic schoolboy to witness a historic event! As the mighty *Vanguard* approached from Fareham Creek she started to head towards Fort Blockhouse, the naval submarine base at Gosport. Obviously the pilot, located way up on the deserted bridge of the huge battleship towering over the harbour, ordered his tugs to correct the swing towards Gosport. This they did but apparently too enthusiastically as the huge hulk swung towards the Portsmouth shoreline."

The tugs' engines churned up the water as they ran hard astern and the skeleton crew released the battleship's anchors in an attempt to check her, but it was in vain as she slid inexorably towards the Custom Watch House and the Still & West public house. Mike continued "The mighty anchor from *Vanguard* not only hit the seabed to slow the ships' forward movement, it also snagged the car ferry chains. For a schoolboy it was an exciting time as two sets of chains entwined rocking the old car ferry from side to side. Perhaps more mature travellers were somewhat more con-cerned, but for schoolboys it was an exciting day out during the long school holidays!"

Members of *Vanguard's* crew waved frantically to the sightseers at Old Portsmouth, warning them to get out of the way as *Vanguard* approached the shore, but many, not realizing the danger, simply waved back. Finally, when she was just ten yards from the shore, *Vanguard* came to rest with her bows firmly embedded in the muddy seabed. Lying in 20 feet of water, her superstructure towering over the buildings of Old Portsmouth, *Vanguard* defied the furious efforts of five tugs to free her for almost an hour, and with the tide beginning to ebb and all traffic in and out of harbour at a standstill, the situation was critical. Suddenly, as if realizing that her fate was inevitable, the battleship slid slowly astern off the mud. She was then led out to Spithead where the ocean-going tugs, *Advice* and *Samsonia*, were waiting to claim her for the passage to the shipbreaker's yard.

On 9 August, five days after leaving Portsmouth, *Vanguard* was towed into the Firth of Clyde where, at the Tail of the Bank, local tugs took the battleship over for the final leg into the Gareloch. She was guided to the pier at Faslane, close to Garelochhead where her final mooring ropes were secured so that shipbreaking could begin. Among the first pieces of equipment to be removed were the 15-inch guns of A and B turrets, together with the mountings which had first gone to sea in 1917, during the Great War.

In all the battleship yielded some 38,800 tons of metal. It was on 2 April 1962 that the last section of her hull, consisting of the double bottom fuel tanks, was towed from Faslane's deepwater berth to the final beaching ground nearby, and by the end of that year she had ceased to exist. For the Royal Navy and, indeed, for naval warfare, it was the end of a tradition that went back to the beginning of the 19th century when the idea of applying armour to warships was first considered. The 20th century had seen the first modern battleship, *Dreadnought*, and now, just 54 years later, came the demise of the Royal Navy's last great leviathan of the seas, *Vanguard*.

The Beginning of the End.......

On the morning of Thursday 4 August 1960, *Vanguard* was towed from her mooring in Fareham Creek bound for shipbreakers at Faslane.

(W. A. Flynn)

As she approached Portsmouth Harbour's narrow entrance the battleship ran aground off Customs Watch House, Old Portsmouth, attracting large crowds of sightseers as the tugs struggled to pull her free. *(W. A. Flynn)*

This aerial shot shows just how close *Vanguard* came to the shore in her reluctance to leave Portsmouth. The crowds outside the Still & West public house can be seen clearly, as can the rows of parked cars in Broad Street. *(W. A. Flynn)*

Tugs struggle to free the battleship for her voyage to the breaker's yard.   *(Imperial War Museum Neg FL20879)*

Once freed *Vanguard* was able to continue her final, one-way, voyage to Faslane. Here the crowds watch in silence as she is towed past Clarence Esplanade.

(Colin Bowden)

On 9 August 1960, five days after leaving Portsmouth, *Vanguard* was towed into the Firth of Clyde, just a few miles from where she was built. At the Tail of the Bank local tugs took over for the final leg into the Gareloch.

(W. H. Rice)

The last few miles as she is slowly towed up Gareloch.

(N. McFarlane)

Vanguard about to berth alongside the shipbreaking berth.   (Ben Warlow)

The day after her arrival at Faslane, and before the demolition process has begun. *(N. McFarlane)*

In early September 1960 X and Y turrets are still intact... *(N. McFarlane)*

But the 15-inch guns of A turret have gone.   *(N. McFarlane)*

..Soon after her arrival at Faslane both the bridge...   *(N. McFarlane)*

...And the upper decks were a shambles.

(N. McFarlane)

An aerial view of *Vanguard* at the Faslane shipbreaking berth of Metal Industries Ltd. All her main armament and her forward funnel have gone, but otherwise she is remarkably intact. *(MoD/Crown Copyright)*

In just a few months, by the spring of 1961 all *Vanguard's* superstructure had been removed and there was little left of the once powerful battleship. *(N. McFarlane)*

102

On 2 April 1962 the final section of *Vanguard*, which consisted of her double bottom tanks, was beached for the last of the demolition work to be completed. Soon afterwards she ceased to exist. *(N. McFarlane)*

Principal Particulars

Dimensions:

Length bp:	760ft
Length oa:	814ft - 4in
Beam:	108ft

Tonnage:

Standard Displacement	44,500
Deep Displacement	51,420
Standard Draught	31ft
Deep Draught	34ft - 10in

Armament:

Eight 15-inch guns: 16 x 5.25-inch guns: 58 x 40mm Bofors: Four 3-pdr saluting guns.

Armour :

Turrets:	13-inch faces: 11-inch sides: 7-inch backs: 4-inch crowns.
Belt::	14-inch over magazines: 13-inch over machinery.
Decks:	6-inch over magazines: 5-inch over machinery.

Main Propulsion Machinery:

Four shafts, powered by Parsons single-reduction geared turbines, 130,000 SHP. Steam provided at 700°F and 400psi by eight Admiralty Three Drum superheated boilers. Fuel 3,800 tons. Speed 30 knots.

Complement:

1,600 (war complement 2,000).

Commanding Officers

Name	Date of Appointment
Captain W. G. Agnew CB CVO DSO	15 October 1945
Captain F. R. Parham DSO RN	29 March 1947
Captain G. V. Gladstone RN	28 July 1949
Captain D. H. Hall-Thompson RN	18 August 1950
Captain J. S. S. Litchfield OBE RN	21 December 1951
Captain R. A. Ewing DSC RN	18 January 1953
Captain Sir St J. Tyrwhitt RN	12 May 1954

Reserve Fleet

Commander H. G. Barnard RN	1 January 1955
Commander J. N. Garnett DSC RN	9 January 1956
Captain A. G. Poe (Senior Officer Reserve Fleet)	1 December 1956
Captain N. W. Fisher (Senior Officer Reserve Fleet)	3 July 1958

Flag Officers in Command

Admiral Sir A. J. Power GCB CBE CVO
C-in-C Mediterranean Fleet.   March 1949

Rear-Admiral E. M. Evans-Lombe CB
Flag Officer Training Squadron, Home Fleet.   August 1949

Admiral Sir P. Vian KCB CB DSO
C-in-C Home Fleet.   September 1950

Rear-Admiral R. M. Dick CBE DSC
Flag Officer Training Squadron, Home Fleet.   May 1951

Admiral Sir G. E. Creasy KCB CB DSO
C-in-C Home Fleet.   January 1952

Admiral Sir M. M. Denny KCB CB CBE DSO
C-in-C Home Fleet.   January 1954

Flag Officers Commanding Reserve Fleet

Vice-Admiral R. G. Onslow CB DSO
28 November 1956

Vice-Admiral G. B. Sayer KCB CB DSC   8 January 1958

Rear-Admiral J. Grant DSO
29 January 1959

Battle Honours

The Armada 1588	Lowestoft 1665
Cadiz 1596	Four Days' Battle 1666
The Kentish Knock 1652	St James' Day 1666
Dungeness 1652	Barfleur 1692
Portland 1653	Quebec 1759
The Gabbard 1653	The Nile 1798
The Texel 1653	Jutland 1916

HMS Vanguard

The Name

The word "vanguard" - derived from the French "avant-garde" - is military rather than naval in origin, and applied to the detachment of an army sent in advance of the main body to guard against any surprise attack. At sea it is used in its abbreviated form "van". The idea of being to the front is implicit in both forms; hence the ship's motto: "WE LEAD".

The Badge

Officially described as "On a field blue, issuing from barry of four white and green a demi-lion gold supporting a spear issuing white."

The badge is an illustration of the ship's name, containing heraldic references to her origin and history: a spearhead, representing the van, is held on guard by a lion, symbolic of Britain's strength; they are shown rising from a sea of white and green, the colours of the House of Tudor in whose time the first ship of the name was built; the lion was also the standard figurehead of the ship of the line of Nelson's day, and is thus a link, though a slender one, between modern ships and Nelson's *Vanguard*, between those who serve today and Nelson.

Former *Vanguards*

The First *Vanguard* 1586-1629

The first *Vanguard* was a 500-ton galleon, which was built on the Thames at Woolwich. She was 108 feet long, with a beam of 32 feet and a depth of 13 feet. She carried an armament of eight demi-cannon (30 pounders), ten culverin (17 pounders), 14 demi-culverin (9 pounders), four light pieces and 18 quick firers. Although *Vanguard* and her sister ship, *Rainbow*, were not the largest warships of their day, in the latter half of the 16th century they were the latest in naval architecture.

Vanguard was commissioned into the Royal Navy when Spain was fitting out her great Armada and massing her armies in the Netherlands for an assault on England. In December 1587 the fleet was ready and waiting for any invasion, and in February 1588 *Vanguard* put to sea to guard against an attempt by the Duke of Parma to cross the Channel from the Netherlands. In May that year, when the main part of the fleet under Lord Howard of Effingham sailed west to meet the Armada, *Vanguard* remained on patrol in the Narrows.

In July 1588, when the Armada arrived in the Western Approaches, *Vanguard* and her squadron maintained the patrol off Dover and, on 29 July, they intercepted a Spanish force off Gravelines. *Vanguard* and *Rainbow* fought the enemy ships at close range and they are credited with having driven ashore two large Spanish ships, the San Felipe and San Mateo.

After the defeat of the Armada *Vanguard* became the flagship of Sir Martin Frobisher, cruising the eastern Atlantic to intercept Spanish convoys which were attempting to reinforce ports on the west coast of France. In 1594 Frobisher's squadron laid siege to the Spanish garrison at Fort Crozon, and during a landing in support of the Army Frobisher himself was fatally wounded. In 1596 *Vanguard* took part in the assault and capture of Cadiz, which resulted in the destruction of much of the Spanish fleet during which she was gainfully employed intercepting a number of enemy vessels which were trying to escape south. Following this *Vanguard* saw no action until 1620 when she formed part of Sir Robert Mansell's force sent to quell Algerian pirates, and she flew the flag of Sir Richard Hawkins (son of the famous Elizabethan, John Hawkins). Finally, in 1629, when she was 43 years old, *Vanguard's* naval career was brought to an end when she was, "cast from the service".

The Second *Vanguard* 1631-1667

The second *Vanguard* was a Second Rate of 731 tons, armed with 58 guns, and with a complement of 500 men. Like her predecessor she was built at Woolwich and she was first commissioned in 1631 for a seven-month voyage escorting merchantmen "southward". In 1633 she was commissioned as the flagship of Sir John Pennington and she carried out patrols in the Channel at which time, although the two countries were not at war, she had the occasional brush with Dutch men o' war. In July 1652 she joined a squadron assembling in the Downs and in the following month she was involved in an indecisive action with a Dutch fleet of 30 ships off Plymouth. On 28 September 1652 she was in action as part of Blake's force against a Dutch fleet off the Kentish Knock shoal. During the battle the Dutch lost several ships and on the following day they withdrew from the battle. A few weeks later, in late November, Blake's fleet, which included *Vanguard*, was again in action against the Dutch off Dungeness during which her ship's company earned the praise of Blake when she went to the aid of *HMS Victory*, which was under attack by a number of enemy ships. Later in the battle she supported Blake's flagship, *Triumph*.

After the battle *Vanguard* was taken in hand for repairs and she was not in service again until January 1653, when she flew the flag of General Monck, "Admiral of the White". In February that year she was in action against the Dutch, this time off Portland, and during the battle she lost her captain and 30 men. She was again mentioned in dispatches as having, "fought with singular dexterity and courage." After the battle *Vanguard* was sent to Portsmouth for repairs, but by 30 March she was back at sea patrolling the south and east coasts to watch for the reappearance of the Dutch fleet.

In June 1653 *Vanguard*, which formed part of Monck's fleet of 100 ships, was in action with a similar sized Dutch force off the Gabbard shoal during which the British ships inflicted a decisive defeat on the enemy, sinking or capturing some 20 vessels. *Vanguard* herself was in the thick of the action continuously, from 11am until sunset on 2 June and from noon until 10pm the next day. Just a few weeks later, on 25 July, Monck's fleet again brought a now much weakened Dutch force to battle off the island of Texel, and this victory for the British fleet forced the Dutch to sue for peace. During the battle, however, *Vanguard* had suffered considerable damage, and it was 1654 before she was at sea again.

In January 1665, with a second Dutch War having broken out, *Vanguard* was in action again, and on 1 June she formed part of the British fleet which engaged the Dutch off Lowestoft during which the enemy lost 30 ships. Two days later, whilst Monck was on passage from the Downs to the Thames, he came upon a Dutch fleet of 85 ships at anchor and despite being outnumbered by the enemy he immediately engaged them. During the next four days the British ships, which included *Vanguard*, were involved in fierce fighting and both sides suffered severe casualties, one of whom was Captain John Whitty of *Vanguard*. On 23 July 1666 *Vanguard* was in action once again at the battle which became known as St James' Day, during which she lost 60 men killed, but captured one ship, sank two and set two others on fire.

In June 1667, however, the Dutch Admiral de With sailed his fleet up the Thames Estuary, and captured the town of Sheerness before continuing up the River Medway. The defenders of the area hastily improvised defences along the river and one of a number of blockships sunk was *Vanguard*, which was scuttled close to Rochester Bridge.

The Third *Vanguard* 1678-1728

Built in 1678, the third *Vanguard* was a Second Rate of 1,357 tons, mounting 90 guns and carrying a complement of 660 men. In May 1692, under the command of Captain Christopher Mason, *Vanguard*, *Victory* and *Duchess* formed part of Sir John Ashby's squadron which, combined with a Dutch fleet, defeated a French force at the Battle of Barfleur. Following this action *Vanguard* was laid up during the winter months as it was inadvisable for a three-decker of those days to face severe winter storms. Each summer, however, she was brought up to full complement and commissioned for service, but she saw no further action. On 27 November 1703, whilst lying in reserve on the Medway, she capsized in a storm and, although she was salved and refitted, she saw no further active service. In 1728 she was renamed *Duke*.

The Fourth *Vanguard* 1748-1774

Although she was, at 1,419 tons, larger than her predecessor, the fourth *Vanguard* carried only 70 guns and she was, therefore, classed as a Third Rate. The Seven Years' War from 1756 to 1763, however, provided her with plenty of action, though it was not until October 1757 that she was sent out from Portsmouth in a squadron under Hawke to intercept a French force of 18 ships, which was returning from Louisburg, French Cape Breton Island. Unfortunately the British ships were dispersed by gale force winds, and when the enemy ships were sighted *Vanguard* was alone. She was engaged by a number of French vessels, but she managed to escape.

Early in 1758 Vanguard was one of a number of warships that were mobilised at Halifax, Nova Scotia, to lay siege to the French base at Louisburg, Cape Breton Island, and she assisted in blockading the harbour. In 1759 *Vanguard* was employed in the lower reaches of the St Lawrence River intercepting any French reinforcements which might be sent to the garrison at Quebec. Here, as at Louisburg, it was a case of landing troops in ships' boats, providing supporting fire for them when ashore, and bombarding the enemy's fixed defences. In addition, ships' guns were landed to reinforce the artillery ashore, and after protracted preliminary diversions and operations came the famous surprise landing and climb to the Heights of Abraham which, on 13 September 1759, resulted in the fall of Quebec to the forces of General James Wolfe. During the winter of 1760, with the French Army laying siege to the British garrison in ice-bound Quebec, *Vanguard* and nine other warships left England to relieve the beleaguered garrison. Arriving off Quebec on 16 May the force quickly sank or drove off the French ships in the river, while *Vanguard* enfiladed the enemy trenches, thus raising the siege and securing the whole of Canada for the British. In the years which followed the relief of Quebec *Vanguard* served in the Caribbean, playing her part in the capture of the islands of Martinique and Grenada. The surrender of the latter in March 1762 marked the end of *Vanguard's* active career and she saw no further action. She was eventually sold out of naval service in 1774.

The Fifth *Vanguard* 1787 - 1821

The fifth, or Nelson's *Vanguard* was a Third Rate of 1,609 tons, armed with 74 guns and carrying a complement of 589. She was completed at Deptford in 1787 and was then laid up in reserve for three years until June 1790 when she commissioned for service with the grand Fleet which was mobilised to provide a show of force during diplomatic negotiations with Spain and Russia. When these were settled amicably she was once again paid off, and she remained in reserve for another two years.

In February 1793, after the outbreak of war with France, she was recommissioned and in June that year she embarked two Regiments of Foot before joining Admiral Lord Howe's fleet at Tor Bay. In the weeks that followed she took part in the blockade of Brest harbour and in late November, together with the frigates *Phoenix*, *Phaeton* and *Latona*, she chased and shared in the capture of the French frigate *La Blonde* off Ushant. However, on 3 December when returning to Devonport, she grounded and had to be dry docked for repairs to her hull. It was January 1794 before she was at sea again, and she arrived in the Caribbean four months later where she formed part of Sir John Jervis' fleet at Martinique. In the summer and autumn of 1794 she took part in the unsuccessful attempt to capture the island of Guadeloupe, and following this combined operation with the Army she returned to naval duties which involved attacking enemy ships and trade, and protecting our own.

The summer of 1795 saw *Vanguard* operating in the Caribbean and in June that year she captured the French corvette *La Pendrix* off Antigua, as well as chasing chased a number of enemy men o' war. In the following year, after pursuing enemy ships, she recaptured *Little Mary*, which had been taken as a prize by the French. Having completed three years on the station, on 14 July 1797 *Vanguard* returned home to the Nore and seven months later she was recommissioned.

On 29 March 1798, at Spithead, she hoisted Admiral Nelson's flag and in the following month she sailed to join St Vincent's fleet off Cadiz. On his arrival off the Spanish coast Nelson was ordered to take *Vanguard* and five other men o' war into the Mediterranean to watch the French fleet in Toulon. Delayed by gales, which caused some damage to his ship, when Nelson finally arrived off the French base he found that the fleet had sailed and his ships were involved in a two-month search for them which eventually yielded success when they were located in Aboukir Bay, 15 miles east of Alexandria. The Battle of the Nile, as it became known, lasted from 6.30pm on 1 August 1798 until almost midnight, when the French flagship, *L'Orient*, blew up with such a violent explosion that men from both fleets were momentarily dazed. By midnight, however, seven enemy ships had been destroyed or captured and next day those that remained were dealt with, until only four of the 17 enemy vessels escaped. It was a stunning victory for Nelson, but the fighting had been fierce and in *Vanguard* alone 30 men were killed and 76 wounded, including Nelson who was hit by a splinter above his blind right eye.

In October that year *Vanguard* was part of Nelson's squadron which blockaded the French garrisons at Malta and Gozo, and in December she evacuated the Neapolitan Royal Family and British Ambassador from Naples to Palermo.

In February 1800 *Vanguard* was paid off and after repairs she recommissioned 12 months later. Shortly afterwards she joined Nelson's force off Copenhagen and service off the Spanish coast followed. In October 1801, when peace treaties were signed, she was withdrawn to Gibraltar and the remainder of her active service was spent in the Caribbean and the Baltic. In November 1811 she was finally paid off at Devonport where she spent the next ten years as a prison and powder hulk until, in 1821, she was broken up.

The Sixth *Vanguard* 1835-1867

Built in 1835 at Pembroke, the sixth *Vanguard* was a Second Rate of 2,609 tons, armed with 80 guns. She had a largely uneventful career, mainly in the Mediterranean, although she took part in some minor campaigns in the Levant. In 1867, with the name *Vanguard* being required for a new battleship, she was renamed *Ajax*.

The Seventh *Vanguard* 1870-1875

The seventh *Vanguard* was built by Cammell Laird & Co at Birkenhead in 1870. She was described as, "an iron central-battery battleship" and her building marked a halfway point in the development of the old wooden sailing ships of the line to the modern battleship. Her guns were arranged in a central battery and, though she was fitted with two steam reciprocating engines which developed 5,312 horsepower, which gave her a speed of 14 knots, she also had three fully rigged masts.

The seventh *Vanguard*, an "iron central-battery battleship" which was sunk in 1875 after a collision with *HMS Iron Duke*.

(Maritime Photo Library)

She was commissioned in 1871 and her short career was spent on the Irish Coastguard Squadron. However, on 1 September 1875, when in the Irish Sea, she was rammed by *Iron Duke* and she sank quickly, but fortunately with no loss of life.

The Eighth *Vanguard* 1908-1917

The eighth *Vanguard*, an improved Dreadnought, was built by Vickers Armstrong at Barrow-in-Furness in 1908, and she was one of three St Vincent-class battleships. She mounted an armament of ten 12-inch guns in three centre line turrets and two twin wing turrets on either side of the ship, as well as a secondary armament of 20, 4-inch guns. Her steam turbine machinery gave her a speed of 21 knots. She was first commissioned at Devonport in 1910 and all her service was with the Home Fleet. In August 1914, on the outbreak of war, *Vanguard* formed part of the 1st Battle Squadron at Scapa Flow, from where she made regular sweeps into the North Sea.

On 30 May 1916 *Vanguard*, which now formed part of the 4th Battle Squadron, sailed on one of Jellicoe's regular sweeps and next day, in the waters of the Skagerrak off the Jutland Peninsular, Scheer's High Seas Fleet was encountered. At 6.30pm the two mighty fleets of Dreadnoughts opened fire as all the theories of a century of peace were put to the test amid the roar of battle and the thunder of the most powerful guns ever fired in anger at sea. Although the Royal Navy lost more men and ships at the Battle of Jutland, the German High Seas Fleet retired to their base at Wilhelmshaven and never put to sea in force again. *Vanguard* was in action from the start until the end of the battle, and she was fortunate in that she suffered neither casualties nor damage.

Vanguard had another year of service with the Home Fleet, but she saw no further action, and on the evening of 9 July 1917, at about 10pm, she was at anchor in Scapa Flow. Suddenly, a massive and violent internal explosion tore the great battleship apart and she sank within seconds. Only 97 members of her 800-strong ship's company survived and, although the precise cause of the explosion was never established, it was almost certainly caused by faulty ammunition.

The eighth *Vanguard*, an improved Dreadnought, was built in 1908 and she mounted a main armament of ten 12-inch guns. On 9 July 1917, whilst at anchor in Scapa Flow, she was destroyed by a massive internal explosion with the loss of over 700 lives.

(Maritime Photo Library)

The Tenth *Vanguard* 1992-

Although she is one of the Navy's capital ships, the ninth *Vanguard* is very different from any of her predecessors, in that she is a nuclear-powered ballistic missile submarine, who has given her name to a class of four such vessels. Laid down in September 1986, *Vanguard* was launched on 4 March 1992 and completed in August 1993. Displacing some 15,000 tons (dived), *Vanguard* is armed with 16 Trident D5 Intercontinental Ballistic Missiles and she is also fitted with four torpedo tubes. She carries a complement of 135 and has a speed of over 25 knots whilst submerged. With her three sisters, *Vengeance*, *Victorious* and *Vigilant*, she forms the spearhead of the United Kingdom's nuclear deterrent.

Acknowledgements

Roger Beacham, Cheltenham Reference Library: Lt Colin Bowden RM (Rtd): Michael Cassar, Valletta, Malta: J. Clarke: D. G. Collins: J. M. Cox: Steve Bush and Mike Critchley, Maritime Books, Liskeard: Lt Norman Curnow RN (Rtd): M. R. Dawe: W. A. Flynn: Derek Fox: Peter Freeman: Peter Harris: R. D. Holdaway: John W. Hucker: Ian Johnston: A. E. Lucas: F. McGuinness: Lt Cdr Joseph. L. Michie RN (Rtd): J. Nixon, University of Glasgow: Tony Perrett, Royal Marines Historical Society: R. J. Poole: Frederick Presswell: Staff of the Public Record Office, Kew: Tony Rees: W. H. Rice: F. W. Russell: E. Skinner: G. Smith: Ian Spashett, FotoFlite, Kent: J. W. Turner: Adrian Vicary, Maritime Photo Library, Cromer: M. J. Wallace: Ben Warlow: J. K. Wilkinson: Finally, to my wife Freda and my daughters Caroline and Louise.